Beginning Quarkus Framework

Build Cloud-Native Enterprise Java Applications and Microservices

Tayo Koleoso

Apress®

Beginning Quarkus Framework: Build Cloud-Native Enterprise Java Applications and Microservices

Tayo Koleoso
Silver Spring, MD, USA

ISBN-13 (pbk): 978-1-4842-6031-9   ISBN-13 (electronic): 978-1-4842-6032-6
https://doi.org/10.1007/978-1-4842-6032-6

Managing Director, Apress Media LLC: Welmoed Spahr
Acquisitions Editor: Steve Anglin
Development Editor: Matthew Moodie
Coordinating Editor: Mark Powers

Cover designed by eStudioCalamar

Cover image by Shahadat Rahman on Unsplash (www.unsplash.com)

Distributed to the book trade worldwide by Apress Media, LLC, 1 New York Plaza, New York, NY 10004, U.S.A. Phone 1-800-SPRINGER, fax (201) 348-4505, e-mail orders-ny@springer-sbm.com, or visit www.springeronline.com. Apress Media, LLC is a California LLC and the sole member (owner) is Springer Science + Business Media Finance Inc (SSBM Finance Inc). SSBM Finance Inc is a **Delaware** corporation.

For information on translations, please e-mail booktranslations@springernature.com; for reprint, paperback, or audio rights, please e-mail bookpermissions@springernature.com.

Apress titles may be purchased in bulk for academic, corporate, or promotional use. eBook versions and licenses are also available for most titles. For more information, reference our Print and eBook Bulk Sales web page at http://www.apress.com/bulk-sales.

Any source code or other supplementary material referenced by the author in this book is available to readers on GitHub via the book's product page, located at www.apress.com/9781484260319. For more detailed information, please visit http://www.apress.com/source-code.

Printed on acid-free paper

*I dedicate this book to my grandma,
who with her grade school education would
constantly implore me to keep studying, up till today.*

*"You know I wasn't a particularly brilliant student;
but you need to be far ahead of me;
never stop your education and passing your exams."*

—Mrs. Cecilia Vincent

Table of Contents

About the Author

Tayo Koleoso is a full-time technical lead and consulting architect with a burning passion for learning, because he knows there's too much he doesn't know, and teaching, because it's the best way to reinforce knowledge. He's an in-person instructor and author, dedicated to topics and technologies he'll have to study religiously to deliver. His journey started from Lagos, in Nigeria, bringing him to the United States as an immigrant software engineer. Across industries, from finance to cybersecurity, he has led teams, architected complicated integrations, and broken and built many fun and mission-critical projects in the enterprise space, with Java and Python, in the cloud. Quarkus is his latest victim.

Outside of technology, he's very passionate about personal finance and the securities market. Throw a couple of habanero peppers in, and he's happy! You can watch and follow his courses on <u>LinkedIn Learning</u>.

About the Technical Reviewer

 **Mouhamadou D. Sylla** is an electrical and software engineer with extensive experience and works for a hi-technology, defense and biomedical research company that provides scientific, engineering, system integration, and technical services. As a senior software engineer, he is responsible for the development integration products produced by the company. Mouhamadou has been working in software development for a decade and has participated and led several development projects in Java. His primary interests include the integration of security into software development lifecycles and emerging technologies such as Quarkus. Mouhamadou graduated from the University of Maryland, College Park, with a BS in Electrical Engineering and minor in Computer Science.

Acknowledgments

I want to thank God, my mother, and sister for all the support and prodding to push this book through.

To my muse and #1 cheerleader, Keni, I say a huge thank you.

My technical reviewer, Mo Sylla, keeping me accurate and on target, thank you so much; it was an honor working on this book with you.

To Eden and her mum, for granting my first book "interview," thank you.

Finally, to the person that set me on this path so many years ago – he probably doesn't even remember – Femi Temowo, thank you so much.

Thanks to the Quarkus crew for building a game-changing platform! Thank you Java for existi... [Cue the walk-off music].

Introduction

Java is dead. Long live Java.

"Cloud-native" is being thrown around in the industry a lot these days; many are joining the "microservice" train as well. Many are not ready. To be truly microservice, cloud-native, or even "cloud-friendly" takes a major mindset shift and technological realignment. Traditional popular Java application design, frameworks, and thinking can no longer deliver the goods.

Quarkus literally puts the "native" in "cloud-native"; this is not your grandma's web service framework.

This book is a view of how Java enterprise applications and microservices will be built and deployed in the future. I've carefully selected the extensions and practices to demonstrate in this text. The intent is to cover the most common use cases in the enterprise, combined with as many easily digestible and functional examples as possible. I aim to demonstrate how to

- Build scalable and cost-effective applications on premises and in the cloud

- Reliably deploy RESTful Java services in the containerized world

- Prepare you and your organization for the architectural and operational changes that are necessary for a successful migration to microservice architecture

- Run resource-efficient Java applications in deployment form factors that were hitherto impractical

- Reuse your existing code and components in the new world of Quarkus

You're not going to want to build Java the old way again. After seeing how much more "performant" your web services can become with the tools in this platform, you'll find there are very few reasons to continue to do Java as of old.

To get the most out of this book you'll need

- Familiarity with Java in an enterprise setting

- A basic understanding of web services

- A basic understanding of the cloud

This book is example-heavy; a lot of the examples can be copy-pasted straight into your IDE and run. Because of the active development going on in this book, it's highly likely that by the time you're reading it, some of it is outdated or functioning differently. This is a good thing: the Quarkus project is *very* actively developed.

After reading this book, you will be able to build and package a production-strength Java application that is natively compiled and deployable on-premise and in the cloud.

CHAPTER 1

Welcome to Quarkus

Quarkus is the latest entrant into the microservice arena, brought to you by our friends over at Red Hat. Now it's not like there aren't enough microservice frameworks out there, but ladies and gentlemen, this one's different. This is one of the precious few microservice frameworks engineered from the ground up for... [drum roll] the cloud.

The market is dominated arguably by the Spring Framework, Spring Boot being its flagship platform for microservices. The Spring Framework does everything and a little more, but one thing needs to be said: its cloud offerings are bolted on; afterthoughts added to a platform born before the era of cloud-*everything*, serverless, and containerization.

Quarkus is a framework built with modern software development in mind, not as an afterthought. It's a platform built to excel as a cloud deployment: as a containerized deployment, inside a stand-alone server, or in one of the common serverless frameworks. Quarkus provides almost everything we've grown accustomed to in a microservice framework like Spring Boot or Micronaut, with a lot of added benefits that put it ahead of the pack. You can run it on-premise, in the cloud, and everywhere in between.

In this chapter, we're going to take a window-shopper look at the framework and even take it for a test drive. Thank you for purchasing this book and choosing to explore this game-changing platform with me.

© Tayo Koleoso 2020
T. Koleoso, *Beginning Quarkus Framework*, https://doi.org/10.1007/978-1-4842-6032-6_1

Write Once, Run ~~Anywhere~~ Predictably (WORP)

Write Once, Run Anywhere (WORA) was the original promise of Java: you write your Java code one time, and it's good to run on any platform where. The way it fulfills that promise is by adding a lot of insulation in the JVM that protects the code from all the peculiarities of various operating systems and platforms. This is intended to mitigate any platform-specific weirdness that might cause code to behave differently.[1] The cost of that insulation is a degradation in the speed of execution, not to mention the bloat in the Java platform code that causes the size of deployment packages to swell considerably. Some even rewrote that aphorism to become "Write Once, Break Everywhere" because among other reasons, once you added application servers to the mix, things got decidedly less predictable.

Enter the age of containerization. Technologies like Docker and VMware Vagrant have rendered the need to write or run insulated code basically unnecessary. Containerization, the cloud, and serverless technology take a lot of the guesswork out of running code. Why should you need to keep yourself guessing what platform your code will be deployed to, when you can reliably deploy to a docker container? You no longer need to "Write Once, Run Anywhere"; you need to "Write Once, Run *Predictably*." WORP code, baby! With a WORP mindset, we can shed all the baggage of insulation that the JDK saddles us with. We can now get much smaller deployment packages. Heck, maybe our code could run a lot *fas-*.

---

[1]The famous "...but it works on my machine?!"

2

Supersonic Subatomic!

Supersonic and *Subatomic* aren't 1980s-era compliments (though Quarkus is totally tubular and radical, dudes and dudettes!). No, it's a tagline that refers to two of Quarkus' biggest differentiators: this framework will usually generate much smaller deployment packages with small memory footprints (subatomic) and deploy faster (supersonic) than most other microservice frameworks on the market.

The folks over at Red Hat mean business with this framework. Quarkus contains most of all the features you've come to expect from a modern microservice framework in a shockingly compact deployment package, a package that's then engineered to start up faster than the competition [*hold for thunderous applause from the serverless crowd*]. It's truly a container-first and cloud-native microservice platform, engineered for

- Fast application startup times to enable quick scaling up or down of applications in a container

- Small memory footprint to minimize the cost of running applications in the cloud

- Predictable deployment scenarios

How is the package so small and fast? The secret sauce is a relatively new Java feature known as *ahead-of-time* (AOT) compilation. A little background on this feature, for the uninitiated (and a trip down memory lane for the platform veterans).

A Brief Primer on JVM Internals

Today's Java is both an interpreted and a compiled language platform. Java started as an interpreted language platform: you save a source file with the `.java` extension and run the javac command to generate a `.class` file. That *class* file contains what's called Java *bytecode*, a java

3

language-specific interpretation of all the java code that you wrote. When you now run "java yourcode.class", the class file is **interpreted** by the JRE into the OS-specific CPU instructions. That intermediate step of translating the class file into CPU-friendly instructions is carried out every time the code is run – every method is reinterpreted for every time it needs to be run. In the modern-day JVM, this would go on for a while, until some methods in your program or chunks of code are marked as "*hotspots*" – meaning the JVM has run these portions of the code many, many times.

At this point, the JVM will then execute a *Just-In-Time* (JIT) compilation of those hotspot portions. The thing is interpretation of the java bytecode slows down the execution; JIT compilation produces durable assembly instructions that can be executed directly by the CPU. This means that there will be no need for the repeat interpretation. As you can imagine, that speeds up those specific parts of the application. The JIT-compiled parts (and only those parts) of the application will become faster to execute than the interpreted parts.

Figure 1-1 illustrates the process.

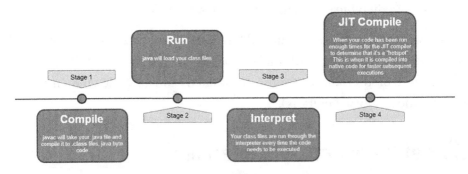

Figure 1-1. *Traditional Hotspot compilation*

Ahead-of-Time Compilation to the Rescue!

Ahead-of-time (AOT) compilation takes compilation further, or rather brings it nearer. AOT compilation takes your `.java` files straight to compiled native binaries that can be immediately executed by the CPU, skipping the relentless interpretation step and passing the savings on to you! Your application starts up significantly faster, and most of the code enjoys the benefit of near immediate computability by the CPU. Additionally, the memory usage drastically shrinks. The performance gains from this process are comparable to what the likes of C++ can boast of. Your entire application, if AOT-compiled, can even become a self-contained executable, without the need for a running, OS-supplied JVM.

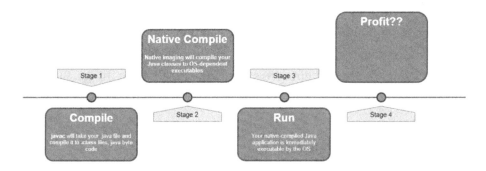

Figure 1-2. *Ahead-of-Time compilation*

But there are a few catches, because there's no free lunch: Quarkus and AOT compilation weave their performance sorcery by stripping the Java runtime to the essentials. Code that's compiled using AOT contains only exactly what that code needs from the JDK, trimming a lot of fat. This upfront compilation step means that it will take a little bit longer than most Java devs are used to. Other time-consuming operations like using the Reflection API are diminished somewhat. For example, if you plan to use reflection, you're going to have to configure your build to prepare to use specific classes reflectively. It's counterintuitive I know, but in practice, it's a minor inconvenience at worst. At best you're guaranteeing the behavior of your application at runtime! *WORP WORP, baby!*

There are some minor sacrifices that are made at the altar of performance that we will examine later in this book. Writing WORP code means deploying predictably. It means knowing what JVM features your application might need ahead of deployment (TLS, Reflection, Injection, etc.). At the end of it all, you're still getting a lot of bang for your buck.

Quarkus Feature Tour

Any good microservice framework must provide a minimum set of features, like running your application without a stand-alone server and opinionated configurations with sensible defaults. Now I'm not going to say that Quarkus is going to make you smarter, wealthier, or more attractive,[2] but I'm also not going to say it won't do all those things. But what *else* can it do?

Native Image Support

As I've mentioned before, a key feature of the Quarkus framework is the ability to generate *native images* from Java code. The native image that's generated skips the interpretation stage of running regular java code, helping it start faster and consume less system resources.[3] The process of generating a native image using AOT strips several layers of "fat" from the JRE and Java code, allowing the finished image to operate with significantly

---

[2]Editor's note: It will not.

[3]The performance gains manifest immediately during startup of the microservice app. There are some special conditions where you may not get the most performance benefits out of the framework, but on the whole, Quarkus is much faster and lighterweight than most of the competition.

less resources than a traditional Java application. This isn't the only mode of Quarkus mind; you can run your Quarkus app as a traditional Java application (so-called JVM mode) without any problems – and still get significant performance boosts. It's just that now, any talk of "Java is too slow to do ${someUseCase}" or "Java is not suitable for embedded deployment" is no longer valid. Cheers to that!

Serverless and Container-Friendly

For the uninitiated, serverless deployment is an application deployment environment available only in the cloud. It's a deployment model that's offered by cloud providers where you don't have to deal with the application server onto which your microservice will be deployed. All you'll need to do as a customer of a serverless-providing vendor is to supply your deployment package – a WAR or in the case of Quarkus, a JAR.

Kubernetes (K8s for short) deployment is a first love for Quarkus – it was designed with K8s in mind, from the container orchestration perspective.[4] With the support for native compilation using GraalVM, Quarkus yields

- Dramatically smaller deployment units

- Much lower memory demands

- Quick startup times

These are factors that you should care about if you're operating in a containerized or serverless environment. You want your dockerized application to start fast and utilize as little RAM as reasonably possible. Why? So that your K8s, Elastic Container Service, or other container management service can quickly scale out your microservice in response

---

[4]Kubernetes is a container management platform that allows you to scale and manage the deployment of a containerized application.

to load. In a serverless scenario, you *really* want your application to start up as quickly as possible; a delay in startup could prove expensive: some cloud providers charge by the amount of time for which a serverless application runs. The native compilation doesn't apply to just your code; many third-party libraries and frameworks that you're used to (Kafka, AWS libraries, etc.) have been engineered using Quarkus' extension API to make them native compilable. This means you can get container-friendly levels of performance out of things like JDBC operations and dependency injection. Even without native compilation, Quarkus as a framework does a lot of upfront optimization to the deployment artifacts that improves startup time. Quarkus ships with in-built support for Amazon Web Services, Azure, and OpenShift.

Hot Reload of Live Code

Developer productivity is another focus of the Quarkus framework. The hot reloading capability in Quarkus allows developers to see their changes to code reflected live. So, when you crack open your favorite IDE (that's right, you get this feature regardless of IDE), and run the project, you don't need to shut down a server or kill the application to see further changes to your code. Simply save the change in the IDE and keep testing the code – no need to restart anything. Even config files! It's pretty awesome to add new dependencies to your Maven POM.xml in a running project and have the new libraries pulled down, all without restarting the app!

Robust Framework Support

Quarkus supports a lot of frameworks out of the box. It also provides a robust extension framework that allows you to add support for your favorite third-party libraries and frameworks. If you've worked with any of

- JavaEE
- MicroProfile

- Apache Camel

- And yes, Spring Framework[5]

you can use all those frameworks inside your Quarkus-based code. As I'll cover in a little bit, Quarkus also covers a lot of the standards we've grown accustomed to: JAX-RS, JAX-B, JSON-B, and so on. It's built to enable fresh microservice development, as well as migrating existing microservices into a Quarkus project. Now as at the time of this writing, Quarkus is still a pretty young platform, so the support for some frameworks is still in preview mode, so your mileage may vary.

Developer-Friendly Tooling

Quarkus provides a rich option set for working with and within the framework. There are feature-rich plugins for both IntelliJ and Microsoft's Visual Studio Code for a GUI-led bootstrapping of a project. There's also the `https://code.quarkus.io/` project starter page, like you get with Spring Boot.

Once you've gotten the project going, there's a healthy ecosystem of extensions that cover most use cases in the microservice world. The *quarkus* Maven plugin gives you handy access to all the functionality you'll need to manage your Quarkus project; my favorite function gives you handy access to plugins just like *Homebrew* (for macOS) and *Node Package Manager* (for Node.js). We see these tools and plugins in action shortly.

---

[5]In preview mode at the time of this writing.

Reactive SQL

Now this one, I got excited when I first read about it. Many facets of Java standard and enterprise programming have gotten the reactive treatment: RESTful service endpoints, core Java,[6] and so on. With Quarkus, database programming is getting the reactive treatment also! Reactive programming as a programming style provides a responsive, flow-driven, and message-oriented approach to handling data. It's designed for high-throughput, robust error handling and a fluent programming style; and it's a very welcome addition to SQL. What does that buy you?

- Being able to operate on database query results as a streaming flow of data, instead of having to iterate over the results one by one

- Processing results of a query in an asynchronous, event-driven manner

- A publish-subscribe relationship between your business logic and the database

- All within a scalable, CPU-efficient, and responsive framework

That's the promise of reactive SQL with Quarkus. As at the time of this writing, only MySQL, DB2 and PostgreSQL support are available in reactive mode in Quarkus.

---

[6]JDK 9 introduced core support for reactive programming with the Flow API, so framework providers can now base their reactive implementations on core java.

Cloud-Native and Microservices-Ready

As anyone who's had to decompose a monolithic application into microservices can attest, it's not a walk in the park. When your architecture is built with the assumption that everything your application will ever need is in a single deployment unit, you're going to find some peculiar challenges breaking it down into microservices. Then double that trouble for pushing the application into the cloud. Quarkus is loaded with extensions that make the transition to microservices a breeze. All of Quarkus' features are in support of a full application living in the highly distributed and disconnected world of the cloud:

- Foundationally, almost everything in Quarkus is reactive for efficient CPU usage and flow control.

- With OpenTracing, MicroProfile Metrics, and Health Checks, you will have eyes and ears over everything your application is doing, especially when a single business process spans multiple independent components "up there," in the sky.

- Your application doesn't have to spontaneously combust every time a black box dependency isn't available for whatever reason: fault tolerance is supported, also via MicroProfile.

JVM Language Support: Scala and Kotlin

Now I'm neither a career Scala programmer nor a Kotlin one, and even I think this is awesome: you can use Quarkus in your Scala and Kotlin projects – and a handful of other JVM-compatible languages! Pretty *hip and with it*, as the kids say.[7]

---

[7]Editor's note: "The kids" haven't said this in over 3 decades. Please stop this.

Getting Started with Quarkus

Red Hat lets you *have it your way* – there are a few options for starting off with a brand new Quarkus project. I'll cover the usual suspects.

Java

Quarkus deprecated JDK 8 support with version 1.4.1 (this book is based on v1.6). The Quarkus team plans to drop support for JDK 8 altogether version 1.6 of Quarkus. It's JDK 11 from there on out.

IDEs

There are plugins for IntelliJ and Microsoft Visual Studio Code; for IntelliJ, go to **File ➤ Settings ➤ Plugins** and search for "Quarkus" and follow the instructions from there. Similarly, for VS Code hit **File ➤ Preferences ➤ Settings** and search for "Quarkus". IntelliJ offers the trademark intuitive interface for starting a project from the Quarkus plugin; my experience with the Visual Studio Code plugin was not as intuitive. Nothing on the Eclipse or NetBeans front as at the time of this writing. Boooo!

Maven

With Apache Maven, you can bootstrap a project from the command line with

```
mvn io.quarkus:quarkus-maven-plugin:1.6.0.Final:create
-DprojectGroupId=com.apress.samples
-DprojectArtifactId=code-with-quarkus
-DprojectVersion=1.0.0-SNAPSHOT
-DclassName=org.acme.ExampleResource
-Dpath=/hello
```

This command uses the `quarkus-maven-plugin`, version **1.6.0.Final** from the `io.quarkus` group. On that plugin, I'm using the `create` goal, passing in additional properties like `className` to generate a REST resource class and `path` to set the path on the REST resource class. The command generates a project named "code-with-quarkus".

The resulting kit is a completely functional application – you can run basic maven commands on it immediately:

```
mvn clean install
```

Quarkus Plugin

The quarkus maven plugin is not your average framework plugin. It's loaded with way more functionality than one would expect. Apart from using it to generate, test, and package a project, you also get to

- Run your project in hot-reload mode with the *dev* goal. In this mode, changes you make to your project's code will be reflected without needing to shut down and restart the application. From within the welcome-to-quarkus directory, run

  ```
  mvn quarkus:dev
  ```

  This starts your Quarkus project in development mode:

  ```
  [io.quarkus] (main) code-with-quarkus 1.0.0-SNAPSHOT
  (running on Quarkus 1.6.0.Final) started in 2.012s.
  Listening on: http://0.0.0.0:8080
       [io.quarkus] (main) Profile dev activated. Live
       Coding activated.
  [io.quarkus] (main) Installed features: [cdi, resteasy]
  ```

Starting Quarkus in dev mode shows you the extensions that are running as the final startup line.

- List the available extensions[8] within the Quarkus ecosystem with the list-extensions goal

```
mvn quarkus:list-extensions
```

This produces a two-column list of all the available extensions you can spice up your application with:

```
Current Quarkus extensions available:
Quarkus - Core                         quarkus-core
JAXB                                   quarkus-jaxb
Jackson                                quarkus-jackson
JSON-B                                 quarkus-jsonb
...
To get more information, append
-Dquarkus.extension.format=full to your command line.

Add an extension to your project by adding the
dependency to your pom.xml or use `./mvnw
quarkus:add-extension -Dextensions="artifactId"`
```

- Add new extensions to your project with the add-extension and add-extensions goals

```
mvn quarkus:add-extension
-Dextension=quarkus-spring-web
```

---

[8]It's important to note that the Quarkus-supplied dependencies you add are not your usual maven third-party libs – they've been engineered to fit into the Quarkus platform, many of them re-engineered to make them compatible for native compilation. They're not your average add-ons.

```
[INFO] --- quarkus-maven-plugin:1.6.0.Final:add-
extension (default-cli) @ code-with-quarkus ---
? Adding extension io.quarkus:quarkus-spring-web
[INFO] ----------------------------------------
[INFO] BUILD SUCCESS
```

The preceding command adds the Spring Web
extension to your project, without you having to go
fish out the maven coordinates yourself. The add-
extension and add-extensions goals will update
the POM.xml file with the Maven details of any
extensions you add without your intervention.

- See a list of available options and other useful
  information with help

```
mvn quarkus:help
```

```
This plugin has 12 goals:
quarkus:add-extension
    Allow adding an extension to an existing pom.xml
    file. Because you can add one or several extension
    in one go, there are two mojos: add-extensions
    and add-extension. Both support the extension and
    extensions parameters.

  quarkus:analyze-call-tree
            Analyze call tree of a method or a
            class based on an existing report
            produced by Substrate when using
            -H:+PrintAnalysisCallTree, and does a more
            meaningful analysis of what is causing a
            type to be retained...
```

Starter Website

For the ultimate in convenience, head on over to code.quarkus.io; point and click your way through to set the multiple attributes about the eventual Maven or Gradle[9] project that it will generate. There, you can also select all the extensions you want to include with the project. The starter page generates a package containing all the basic project files.

Quarkus Maven Project Kit

Whichever approach you take to bootstrap, your generated project should contain at least the following:

- The standard Java project directory structure: src/main/java, src/main/test, src/main/resources, pom.xml, README.md

- Docker artifacts: src/main/docker/Dockerfile.jvm, src/main/docker/Dockerfile.native

- Property file for holding application configuration properties: src/main/resources/application. properties

- An informational page that you can just delete if you don't want it in your setup: src/main/META-INF. resources/index.html

---

Tip   Use the quarkus:generate-config maven goal to generate an application.properties file that contains all available Quarkus framework properties, all disabled. With this, you can have a look at what's available to be configured.

---

[9]Gradle support is in preview mode.

You can go ahead and bootstrap your project; run

```
mvn quarkus:dev
```

to start the project, without adding any code. Navigate to localhost:8080 and you should see the Quarkus welcome page as shown in Figure 1-3.

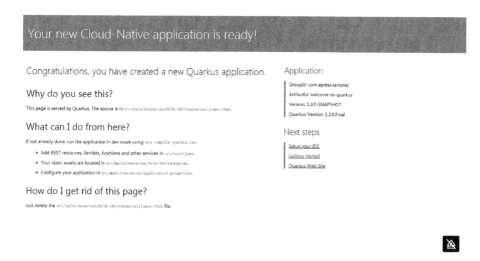

Figure 1-3. *Quarkus app landing page[10]*

Quarkus Main Class

If you're coming from the Spring Boot world, you're probably used to having a main method that starts running your application. Quarkus doesn't require that; it implicitly uses io.quarkus.runner.GeneratedMain as the default main class, so you generally don't have to write a custom one. If you must have control of the launch of your Quarkus application, you have a couple of options, but just one of them is really worth the candle:

---

[10]Yeah, it says v1.2, but that's just because they haven't gotten around to updating this page in a while.

```java
import io.quarkus.runtime.Quarkus;
import io.quarkus.runtime.QuarkusApplication;
import io.quarkus.runtime.annotations.QuarkusMain;

@QuarkusMain (1)
public class CustomQuarkusRunner {

    public static void main(String[] args) {
        Quarkus.run(args);
    }

    public static class StartupHandler implements
    QuarkusApplication {
        @Override
        public int run(String... args) throws Exception {
            customStartupHandler(args);
            Quarkus.waitForExit();
            return 0; //or 1, depending on the termination
            conditions
        }

        public static void customStartupHandler(String[]
        parameters) {
            //handle parameters or Quarkus.asyncExit();
        }
    }
}
```

It's really a combination of two separate approaches:

1. I mark my CustomQuarkusRunner class with
   @QuarkusMain to flag it to the Quarkus runtime as
   a bootstrap class. The Quarkus team recommends
   against performing any heavy-duty processing
   directly inside the main method.

2. Instead, I provide a different class that implements the `QuarkusApplication` interface. It's inside the run method of this interface I'm expected to do my heavy lifting. It could be something as simple as validating the input supplied as command-line parameters. If things don't look right, I can call the `Quarkus#asyncExit` method, which will attempt a graceful shutdown.

3. I can then use `Quarkus#waitForExit` to listen for termination signals from any source.

You can get a hold of the command-line parameters anywhere else inside your application with

```
@Inject
@CommandLineArguments
String[] commandLineArgs;
```

This now makes your Quarkus app a viable candidate for a purely command-line interface (CLI) app. Otherwise, to run your project in production mode, use good ol' Java. First build the project with Maven:

```
mvn install
```

When that completes successfully, from the project folder, run the completed project with vanilla Java:

```
java -jar target/code-with-quarkus-1.0.0-SNAPSHOT-runner.jar
```

And that's it.

And let me tell you, I certainly felt more attractive after experimenting with Quarkus, so take that, editors! So come watch me fill out the guts of my Quarkus project with a bunch of neat tools and best practices, over the next couple of chapters! By the end of this book, you too will look and feel even more stunning than you already do.

CHAPTER 2

Dependency Injection

As the old saying goes, "Teach a man to fish, and dependency injection will keep fresh fish coming,"[1] dependency injection is the lifeblood of any serious enterprise Java application.

Dependency injection (DI) is the mechanism by which java objects are made available at specific points in your code by the *runtime*. It's an implementation of the inversion of control (IoC) design pattern that makes it so that application code can be loosely coupled. So instead of non-DI code:

```
MyDependency myDependency = new MyDependency();
//some business logic
myDependency.cleanUp();
myDependency = null;
```

you can have DI code:

```
@Inject
MyDependency myDependency;
```

The @Inject annotation indicates to the *runtime* that an instance of MyDependency needs to be available, *stat*! You don't need to worry about how the object is instantiated, destroyed, or anything in between. There's quite a bit more to the topic and the mechanism, but that's out of the scope

---

[1]Editor's note: Not how that saying goes. You could have googled this.

© Tayo Koleoso 2020
T. Koleoso, *Beginning Quarkus Framework*, https://doi.org/10.1007/978-1-4842-6032-6_2

of this book. Suffice it to say that behind the scenes, a DI *runtime* provides a service to you: providing you objects wherever you need them. There are a few DI runtimes, and these are the top three in the Java ecosystem:

- Contexts and Dependency Injection

- Spring Framework (*obviously*)

- Google Guice

Figure 2-1. *Pictured: Dependency Injection*

Quarkus provides support for the first two DI frameworks. *Supersonic Subatomic* code that runs like greased lightning doesn't *fully* implement all available DI functionality. Full-fledged dependency injection requires *a lot* of guesswork and usage of the JDK's Reflection API. All of that gets expensive with a full-fledged DI implementation, so the Quarkus team made smart, intuitive decisions about what to support and what not to support. But, fear not: where Quarkus closes a window, it opens a door. Any functionality that's had to be jettisoned, more than likely has a suitable replacement elsewhere in the Quarkus extensions ecosystem.

Contexts and Dependency Injection

Contexts and Dependency Injection (CDI) is the standard DI framework for the Java ecosystem, derived largely from Red Hat's *Seam* framework. Note that I said framework. CDI is a JavaEE specification, officially called JSR 365. What this means is that Java platform vendors like Red Hat, Google, Spring, and others are free to implement their own interpretation of CDI. This is what the Quarkus team at Red Hat has done in developing ArC, the DI runtime built specifically for use in Quarkus.

Getting Started with CDI

Before we get into the meat of things with Quarkus, you should get a fundamental understanding of the DI framework on which everything is built. This isn't going to be a deep dive into CDI. I'm going to show you only just enough CDI for you to have a good time building Quarkus applications. Hope you've brought an appetite, because we're about to get into some beans!

```java
@ApplicationScoped (1)
@Named("deliciousVanilla") (2)
public class VanillaBean implements FlavorTown{
    long flavorStrength;
    String countryOfOrigin;
    //other "stuff"
}
```

This is a "vanilla" CDI bean with

1. A scope: "Application" scope here

2. A name: "deliciousVanilla"

And that's really all it takes for a class to be known to CDI as a bean, in Quarkus.[2] Give it a scope *or* a name – with the @Named annotation. You can then use this bean in *another* bean like so:

```
@RequestScoped (1)
public class VanillaCake{
    @Inject (2)
    @Named("deliciousVanilla")
    VanillaBean vanillaBean;
    @Inject
    FlavorTown aFlavor; (3)
}
```

Here's what's going on here:

1. I'm using a different scope here, a narrower one – the request scope.

2. Then I inject my VanillaBean into this class, using the bean's name as a qualifier.

3. I can also just inject the same bean, without specifying a name or any kind of qualifier. Because VanillaBean is annotated with @ApplicationScoped, there's only ever going to be one instance of it in the entire context. So, aFlavor == vanillaBean will be true.

Note that @Named is optional – it's just a qualifier you can do without in many situations. Also notice how I don't have any getters or setters in there, against the JavaBean convention? That's because it's not necessary for injection in CDI. @Inject can also supply instances to methods:

---

[2]Plain CDI, like as you would find in a Jakarta EE application server like GlassFish, actually doesn't even require @Named or a scope annotation. Quarkus is more restrictive for performance reasons.

```
@Inject
public void gimmeSomeFlavor(FlavorTown flavor){

    ...

}
```

There's also the @Context annotation. Use this annotation to obtain instances of certain specialized components from the JavaEE world. There's a little bit of overlap between @Context and @Inject. There's currently talk about deprecating @Context in favor of @Inject. For what it's worth, @Context supplies REST components that @Inject doesn't currently supply,[3] so it still has its uses. If you have bean classes packaged in a JAR, add a file named *beans.xml* (more on this shortly) to the META-INF directory of the package and CDI will find and supply the beans present in that JAR.

Bean Scopes

All you need to know about bean scopes is that they determine how long your bean will live. They also determine how many instances of your bean will be available at any given time. For the purposes of "Quarkusing," here are the scopes that matter in increasing order of lifespan:

1. @Dependent: Beans with this annotation don't have a lifespan of their own. They last as long as their injection target. For example, inject a @Dependent bean into an @ApplicationScoped bean, then the @Dependent bean lives as long as the @ApplicationScoped bean.

---

[3]Check out my LinkedIn Learning video on this very topic.

2. @RequestScoped: Beans with this annotation are created anew for every request to your web service. This means that two injections of the same @RequestScoped bean will get two different instances of that same bean.

3. @ApplicationScoped: A bean with this scope will be maintained for the entire uptime of the application. *There can only be one.*

4. @Singleton: This technically isn't a scope – it's a stereotype. In addition to limiting a bean to a single instance within the application, this annotation can get special treatment regarding transactions and locking, for example. For Quarkus' purposes though, it's functionally identical to @ApplicationScoped.

There are a couple of other scopes that are recommended in the CDI specification. They're not here in the hall of fame, because they have no relevance in a non-web application framework like Quarkus. So, suck it, scopes not invited to the party!

Producer and Disposer Methods

A CDI producer method lets you take control of the process of instantiating a CDI bean. Check this out:

```
@Produces
@Named("boldVanilla")
@RequestScoped
public VanillaBean vanillaBean(){
    VanillaBean vanillaBean = new VanillaBean();
    vanillaBean.setFlavorStrength(30);
    vanillaBean.setCountryOfOrigin("Madagascar");
return vanillaBean;
}
```

With that method defined in any class, managed bean or not, the following injection will obtain its bean instance from my producer method. The optional @Named qualifier and @RequestScoped I've supplied there will also kick in at the injection site. With those two annotations, I've defined the default name and scope of the VanillaBean. I can override the name the bean at the point of injection, as well as set my desired scope before injection:

```
@Inject
@Named("boldVanilla") @ApplicationScoped
VanillaBean vanillaBean;
```

Producer methods are particularly useful when you want to supply non-managed beans, using CDI and managed bean components. Say you need to provide a third-party class with some preconfigured variables, you use a producer method.

The "destructive" counterpart to a producer method is the *disposer* method:

```
public void compostVanillaBean(@Disposes VanillaBean
vanillaBean){
    Composter composter = new Composter();
    composter.compost(vanillaBean);
}
```

This method will be called by the CDI runtime whenever instances of VanillaBean need to be destroyed. I get to do my cleanup here before the bean goes kaput.

Caution   A disposer method must be matched by a corresponding producer method returning the same class. Without a matching producer method, you will get a deployment exception. A producer method on the other hand doesn't require a disposer method.

You can also get information about the destination where the produced bean is to be injected, with javax.enterprise.inject.spi. InjectionPoint:

```
@Produces
@Named("selectiveVanilla")
@RequestScoped
public VanillaBean vanillaBean(InjectionPoint injectionPoint){

    ...
    injectionPoint.getType().getTypeName(); //the name of the
                                           injection class
    injectionPoint.getMembers() //other fields in the injection
                            class
    injectionPoint.getQualifiers()//qualifier annotations on
                            the injection site
...

}
```

With these and all the other metadata available, you can build conditional logic around what your producer method delivers for injection. A producer method is also a fine option to inject lists of beans into your application. Go nuts!

Quarkus doesn't require @Produces on producer methods; I just prefer it for completeness and conformity with the CDI specification – and also because I like to type words.

Qualifiers

CDI provides *qualifiers*: custom annotations you can apply to your managed beans that further help to distinguish them from other beans. So, given these two beans

```
@ApplicationScoped
public class VanillaBean implements FlavorTown{
  ...
}
@ApplicationScoped
public class BeaverVanilla implements FlavorTown{
  ...
}
```

the following injection will fail:

```
@Inject
FlavorTown beaverVanilla;
```

You will get an error message like

```
Ambiguous dependencies for type [FlavorTown] with qualifiers
[@Default] at injection point
```

This happens because the ArC CDI engine wouldn't know which implementation of FlavorTown it needs to deliver. I need to create a qualifier that further distinguishes the class that I'm interested in injecting:

```
@Qualifier
@Retention(RUNTIME)
@Target({METHOD, FIELD, PARAMETER, TYPE})
public @interface Rare{}
```

A qualifier is just any custom annotation that itself is annotated with @Qualifier. With this annotation, I can designate one of my FlavorTown bean classes as "rare":

```
@ApplicationScoped
@Rare
public class BeaverVanilla implements FlavorTown{
  ...
}
```

I've now designated BeaverVanilla[4] as a special implementation, by applying my @Rare qualifier:

```
@Inject
@Rare
FlavorTown beaverVanilla;
```

This injection will sail right through! The CDI engine will know the specific implementation of FlavorTown I'm interested in injecting. For what it's worth, CDI supplies a number of implicit qualifiers out of the box, as does Quarkus. For example, @Named is a fine qualifier for many use cases.

Bean Configuration File

The CDI spec mandates a file named "beans.xml" as the configuration file for establishing CDI functionality in a Java application. Making this file available within a project, even without configuration, is what kick-starts the CDI runtime. It's this file that will cause the classpath to be scanned and all the managed bean annotations picked up. Here's what it looks:

```
<?xml version="1.0" encoding="UTF-8"?>
<beans xmlns="http://xmlns.jcp.org/xml/ns/javaee"
       xmlns:xsi="http://www.w3.org/2001/XMLSchema-instance"
       xsi:schemaLocation="http://xmlns.jcp.org/xml/ns/javaee
       http://xmlns.jcp.org/xml/ns/javaee/beans_2_0.xsd"
       bean-discovery-mode="all" version="2.0">
</beans>
```

Since JavaEE 7 however, this file is no longer necessary for the runtime bootstrap. You now need it only for advanced configuration of managed beans.

---

[4]Fun fact: A very small percentage of the world's vanilla supply comes from beavers. Please don't ask what part of the beaver produces the vanilla.

Aspect-Oriented Programming

CDI provides some aspect-oriented programming to support implementing cross-cutting concerns. Thankfully, CDI dispenses with the fancy AOP lingo, and it's all boiled down to two components:

- Interceptor binding

- Interceptor

Now stay with me: I'll start with the interceptor binding. The interceptor binding is the annotation I'll use to mark methods that you want to apply cross-cutting concerns to:

```
@Inherited (1)
@InterceptorBinding (2)
@Retention(RUNTIME)
@Target({METHOD, TYPE})
public @interface Audited{
}
```

1. @Inherited makes it so that this annotation can be inherited by child classes.

2. @InterceptorBinding is what really makes this an interceptor binding. Interceptor bindings can declare interceptor bindings as well. That way, you can combine more cross-cutting concerns in fewer annotations.

I have the annotation, now for the class that will execute the cross-cutting concern – the *Interceptor* [lightning and thunder sound effects]:

```
@Audited (1)
@Interceptor (2)
@Priority(Interceptor.Priority.APPLICATION)(3)
public class AuditingInterceptor implements Serializable {
```

31

```
...
@AroundInvoke (4)
public Object logExecutions(InvocationContext
invocationContext) throws Exception {
    logger.info("Method: "+ invocationContext.getMethod().
    getName()); (5)
    logger.info("Arguments: "+invocationContext.
    getParameters());
    logger.info("Executing the called method");
    Object possibleReturn = invocationContext.proceed(); (6)
    logger.info("The object the method was invoked on:
    "+invocationContext.getTarget());
    return possibleReturn;
}
}
```

Alrighty then, let's dig in:

1. I apply my previously created @Audited interceptor binding. This is how this annotation will become effective as an AOP annotation.

2. @Interceptor marks this class as an interceptor.

3. @Priority gives this interceptor a numerical rank, relative to other interceptors. The Interceptor. Priority enum contains some presets, but any integer will do.

4. The @AroundInvoke annotation will cause this method to be invoked whenever a method with @Audited is invoked. An interceptor class can have any number of @AroundInvoke methods; they will all be executed in order of appearance in the class.

5. I get the `javax.interceptor.InvocationContext` which gives me information about the intercepted method.

6. I **must** call proceed on the `InvocationContext`, to ensure that the intercepted method gets invoked.

All I need to do now is apply my annotation wherever I want the auditing:

```
@ApplicationScoped
public class Generator{
    ....
    @Audited
    public String generateAnagram(String source){
        logger.info("Generatin'");
        ...
    }
}
```

ArC CDI Engine

In older versions of Quarkus, you would have had to add ArC support to your Quarkus microservice, using the `quarkus-arc` extension. Now, it's bundled with the core of the framework.

Getting Started with ArC

Now, I'm showing this only for completeness of information. I'm not a big fan of tight coupling with frameworks – JavaEE standards exist for a reason,[5] and we live in a society, dang it! You can directly access the

---

[5]That reason being flexibility: Better to use JavaEE standard annotations, instead of implementation-specific constructs for portability and predictability of behavior.

ArC (and by *extension*, CDI) context from a Quarkus extension or your managed bean using `io.quarkus.arc.ArcContainer` – from within a managed bean

```
ArcContainer arcContainer = Arc.container();
```

This is the ArC way of gaining access to the CDI runtime. It gives you access to the `BeanManager`, among other core pieces of the CDI runtime. In the CDI world, the `BeanManager` is the gateway to all the beans and scopes available in the context. You can use it to create, search, and destroy all available beans within the context.

As I've talked about, there are three main avenues to inject or obtain resources:

- `@Inject`

- `@Context`

- Producer methods and fields

Generally, you'll use `@Inject` to supply objects of your own custom classes. You need the `@Context` annotation to deliver some specialized, container-managed objects that you're not in control of. Go check out the latest version of the CDI specification to see a complete list of specialized objects that are available to you, courtesy of the CDI runtime. To be safe, I recommend adding the `quarkus-undertow` extension to your microservice:

```
mvn quarkus:add-extension -Dextension=quarkus-undertow
```

This increases the variety of container-managed components you can inject; Undertow brings with it several servlet-related components like `org.jboss.resteasy.spi.HttpRequest` and `javax.servlet.ServletContext`, among others:

```
@Inject
ServletContext servletContext;

@Inject
HttpRequest httpRequest;
```

Note how I'm using @Inject to deliver the ServletContext object here; that's a personal preference that I recommend for you too, in preparation for a probable retirement of the @Context annotation in the future.

Heads Up   Quarkus and its native image generation performs better CDI work without private members. Dependency injection requires a lot of Reflection API usage, which is very expensive. In the interest of generating better-performing native images, don't use the private modifier for fields. Stick with package-level access for class-level variables.

Quarkus-Only Enhancements to CDI

Quarkus enriches its implementation of CDI in ArC, by adding the following features, among others.

Lazy Bean Initialization

All the bean initializations are lazy by default. So, given an @ApplicationScoped bean like this

```
@ApplicationScoped
public class StartupConfigCheck {
    Logger logger = Logger.getLogger(StartupConfigCheck.class.
    getName());
```

```
@PostConstruct
public void startupOperations(){
    //heavy lifting startup business logic
}
@PreDestroy
public void shutdownOperations(){
    //here goes your shutdown business logic
}
}
```

the heavy lifting I'm doing in the @PostConstruct method will not kick in until the first time the bean is injected anywhere in the application. In standard CDI behavior where all the beans are instantiated at startup, your application could pay an unnecessary startup time cost due to long-running initialization operations.

Tip   You can still force eager initialization with the **io.quarkus. runtime.Startup** annotation applied to the bean class. Be sure to not confuse this one for the javax.ejb.Startup annotation that does the same thing, but only for Enterprise JavaBeans (EJB).

Custom Lifecycle Events

You get the io.quarkus.runtime.StartupEvent and io.quarkus. runtime.ShutdownEvent classes to hook into the ArC runtime's startup and shutdown steps, respectively. Here's what that looks like:

```
@ApplicationScoped
public class StartupConfigCheck {

    ...
```

```
public void startupOperations(@Observes StartupEvent
startup){
    //here goes your startup business logic
}
public void shutdownOperations(@Observes ShutdownEvent
startup){
    //here goes your shutdown business logic
}
}
```

The @Observes annotation will be used to deliver these event objects where necessary. Beans that contain StartupEvent and ShutdownEvent listeners will eagerly be instantiated. They trigger this behavior regardless of the scope of the parent CDI bean.

Default Beans

What's a @DefaultBean? It's an annotation that lets you set a bean to be a default option, in case of injections. It's a little weird to explain, easier to show. Here's a producer method:

```
@Produces
@RequestScoped
@Named("simpleBatchProcessWorker")
@DefaultBean
public BatchProcessWorker customComponentProvider(){
    return new SimpleBatchProcessWorker();
}
```

This producer method guarantees that there will always be an instance of BatchProcessWorker available for injection. When there isn't any available source of BatchProcessWorker anywhere else in the Quarkus code, io.quarkus.arc.DefaultBean will step in and supply the default. If another implementation exists, that implementation takes precedence.

Conditional Bean Supply

Use io.quarkus.arc.profile.IfBuildProfile and io.quarkus.arc.
DefaultBean to programmatically control when a bean is loaded. Check
this out:

```
public class BeanSupplier{
    @Produces
    @IfBuildProfile("test-east")(1)
    public BatchProcessWorker eastRegionCustomComponent
    Provider(){
        return EastOnlyBatchProcessWorker();
    }

    @Produces
    @UnlesBuildProfile("prod")
    public BatchProcessWorker testingOnlyBean(){
        ...
    }

    @Produces
    @DefaultBean (2)
    public BatchProcessWorker customComponentProvider(){
        return new SimpleBatchProcessWorker();
    }
}
```

Here's the voodoo going on:

1. This producer method will deliver a
   EastOnlyBatchProcessWorker only if the Quarkus
   application is deployed with the "test-east" profile active.
   Conversely, Quarkus provides the @UnlessBuildProfile
   annotation to exclude a specific profile. With
   @UnlessBuildProfile("exclude-me"), the annotated
   bean or producer method will be activated *unless* the
   profile named "exclude-me" is active.

2. Without the expected profile being active, the
    customComponentProvider producer method kicks
    in and supplies a SimpleBatchProcessWorker as the
    default bean.

Lean Bean Cleaning Machine

Quarkus removes unused beans from the DI runtime during startup. This
leaves the runtime lightweight without any unnecessary beans to track.

Tip   Add quarkus.log.category."io.quarkus.arc.
processor".level=DEBUG to the application.properties
file. This enables debug-level logging specifically for ArC. With this,
you can see all the optimizations ArC is doing during startup. A bonus
is that you can see all the unused CDI-injectable beans that ArC
removes from the runtime. Even more bonus: It shows you what you
can inject in the ArC world.

---

beans.xml

beans.xml is not required to activate dependency injection in Quarkus,
contrary to the CDI specification. The only scenario where this file will
become necessary is when you package bean classes in an archive like a
JAR, and you need those beans available in your Quarkus app. Packaging a
beans.xml file in such an archive will expose those beans to ArC and make
them injectable.

Limitations of ArC

If you're new to CDI, just skip this bit. You don't know what you're missing; and you'll find that you don't need those things anyway. If you're already a CDI veteran, know ye this: ArC can do most things as stipulated by JSR-365, but there are some things that it doesn't do, mostly by design. Remember, Quarkus is in the business of speed and predictability; some CDI features just don't jive with that:

- No @ConversationScoped beans, or "passivation-capable" beans:[6] This should mean no beans that implement Serializable or beans that will require serialization to a file. But Quarkus supports the CDI @SessionScoped, a passivation-capable bean. Curious.

- As the contents of beans.xml are ignored,

  - No CDI portable extensions: The Quarkus extension framework is all the extension framework you'll need. Trust me, vanilla CDI extensions are overweight and suboptimal for the tier of performance Quarkus aims for.

  - No beans.xml-based ordering of @Alternative beans; and you don't need it: Quarkus provides io.quarkus.arc.AlternativePriority, an annotation that designates a bean as an alternative, as well as assigns a numerical priority.

- No CDI's Specialization with @Specializes: But @Specializes is just an alternative that allows inheritance of CDI qualifiers. For a replacement, consider programmatically inheriting the available

---

[6]Passivation-capable beans as defined in the CDI specification.

qualifiers. An alternative approach is to dynamically modify the qualifiers at the injection point, guaranteeing that the desired implementation is injected. This can be achieved with the Quarkus extension framework.

- No CDI decorators: You won't be able to delegate functionality to custom beans using @Decorator and @Delegate.

Spring Framework

Ah yes, the beloved Spring Framework. It's a behemoth platform that does a lot for the developer and the enterprise; Quarkus on its own is not a replacement for Spring Boot.Yet. That feature parity comes with Apache Camel. If you aren't familiar with the Apache Camel Framework, I can't recommend it enough. So much so that, I've had colleagues that call me "Mr. Camel"; even going as far as saying I share similarities with them! How cool is that?. Apache Camel opens up a world of options for integrating with many, many systems. With that in your stack, Quarkus could easily rival Spring. The Apache Camel team has even forked off their project into a branch focused on porting Camel extensions for Quarkus support.

Don't get me wrong, the Spring Framework is an awesome project; *but,* if you want to try Quarkus out and still want to leverage the investments you've made in Spring, this section is for you. This section is about showing where Quarkus integrates elements of the Spring Framework. There are features that are already easily reproducible with ArC. This bit is so that you can drop in your existing Spring-based beans and configuration into the Quarkus world. But really, check out this gorgeous fella:

Figure 2-2. *"Meow" – This handsome camel,[7] probably*

Wait, what? What do you mean that's not a camel?

Figure 2-3. *Camel*

Oh. Well that's just cr-

---

[7]Editor's note: Not a camel.

Quarkus Spring Annotation Support

Quarkus provides support for annotations from the following Spring projects. What this means is that you can bring in most of the annotations from these projects and more, and they'll behave the way you expect them to. It's important to understand that under the hood, it's Quarkus that's providing the services of these annotations, not the Spring framework. These are some of the Spring modules supported. Visit the Quarkus website for an up to date list of supported modules - they're always adding more:

- Spring Core

- Spring Web

- Spring Security

- Spring Data JPA

- Spring Boot Properties

I'll add the core Spring Framework support extensions to my Quarkus app:

```
mvn quarkus:add-extension -Dextension=spring-di
```

Pro Tip   Remember, the `list-extensions` Maven goal will show you all the available extensions in the Quarkus ecosystem; they're always adding more. `add-extension` will install the latest version too.

Mixing Beans

"Quarkus provides support for annotations" is an intentional statement: Quarkus will recognize the documented Spring annotations and interfaces. Then using ArC, it can provide the required services and functionality. What this means is that you can bring the following bean into a Quarkus project:

43

```
@Controller
@RestController
@RequestMapping
public class SpringController{
    @Autowired
    private AnotherSpringBean linkedBean;

    @Autowired
    ValueObjectRepository<ValueObject, Long> springJpa;

}
```

and Quarkus + ArC will provide the required REST endpoint, Spring
Boot JPA repository and injections, like nothing's changed. Your Spring
configuration bean can also just be transplanted:

```
@Configuration
public class AppConfiguration {
    @Bean(name = "anotherSpringBean")
    public AnotherSpringBean anotherSpringBean() {
        return new AnotherSpringBean();
    }
}
```

That, however, is the extent of the Spring Framework support as at the
time of this writing. In Quarkus, there is no Spring ApplicationContext to
access, nor are there Spring context-based services available.

As you'll see later chapters in this book, Quarkus has its own Jakarta EE
and MicroProfile-based support for web services, security, data access,
configuration, and so much more. The support for these annotations
in Quarkus is partly an avenue to encourage and support transition of
existing Spring applications into Quarkus. That bears repeating: Quarkus
is cool with your *precious* Spring Framework annotations, but it doesn't
need them. So, you won't be able to use org.springframework.context.

ApplicationContextAware to key into the Spring context; nor will you be able to process Spring context events. But you get to combine two very powerful sets of annotations! Think about it: Spring and CDI beans combined and seen as one! Check it out, it's awesome:

```
@Named("aCdiBean")
@ApplicationScoped
public class CdiDao implements AnagramDao{
    @Autowired
    AnotherSpringBean springBean;

     ...
}
```

Given a Spring-annotated AnotherSpringBean, I can inject it into a CDI-annotated CdiDao. I can also put a CDI-annotated bean into the Spring-annotated one:

```
@Controller
@RestController
@RequestMapping
public class SpringController{
    @Autowired
    @Qualifier("aCdiBean")
    AnagramDao aCdiBean;

     ...
}
```

Yeah, that's right. Spring's @Qualifier is equivalent to CDI's @Qualifiers, including @Named. What else would you need to bring Spring beans into the CDI world?

Substitute ApplicationContextAware and BeanFactory

And again, *not a fan* of too close a coupling to framework code, but there are CDI-based approaches to Spring functionality. The most common direct developer use of org.springframework.context. ApplicationContextAware is to access the Spring ApplicationContext. Many ApplicationContext features are reproducible in CDI. The fundamental use of the ApplicationContext is to directly access Spring beans. Here's how you get a hold of a specific bean in CDI:

```
@Inject
BeanManager beanManager; (1)
...
public void getBean(){
    Bean namedCdiBean = null; (2)
    HashSet<Bean<?>> beans = (HashSet<Bean<?>>) beanManager.
    getBeans("aSpringOrCdiBean"); (3)
    if(!beans.isEmpty()){
        namedCdiBean = beans.iterator().next(); (4)
            CreationalContext creationalContext = beanManager.
            createCreationalContext(namedCdiBean); (5)
            ASpringOrCdiBean bean= (ASpringOrCdiBean)
            beanManager.getReference(namedCdiBean,namedCdiBean.
            getBeanClass(),creationalContext); (6)
            }
    }
}
```

It's a fair bit more typing than what you're probably used to, if you're coming from Spring. If you're new to this, stay with me and let's walk through the steps:

1. I obtain an injection of the `BeanManager` object. There's only one, just like the `ApplicationContext` in the Spring Framework.

2. Before I can get a hold of a named bean, I start with the generic `Bean` interface.

3. I then use the `BeanManager` to search for and retrieve the CDI bean by name.

4. If the search is successful, I simply pick up the first and only item in the set.

5. Each CDI bean is associated with a context, but here's where things differ from Spring. In the CDI world, beans and the context are somewhat disconnected. In Spring, the context is tightly coupled with the beans. Way more flexibility in CDI is what I'm saying. For that reason, I need to manufacture a `CreationalContext` object, to obtain a contextually valid reference to the bean I'm interested in.

6. Finally, I use the `BeanManager` and the `CreationalContext` to retrieve the bean from the generic `Bean` container object.

I'll admit, it's more typing than one should *want* to do, but come on: you really should only have to do this occasionally. `@Inject` wherever you need your beans. The `BeanManager` sort of combines the features of Spring's `ApplicationContext` and the `org.springframework.beans.factory.BeanFactory` interface. With the `BeanManager` however, you've got a nice, healthy bowl of mixed Spring and CDI beans. Yum!

Substitute Spring Application Events

Yes, CDIs got you covered here too. There are fancier, more high-performing ways to handle inter-bean messaging in Quarkus, but here's how you do it with raw CDI.

As with any event-driven design, there are two parts to the operation: firing the event and observing the event. Have a seat; I'll start with firing the event.

Fire CDI Events

Well, I need the event data to send first, don't I?

```
public class InterestingEvent{
    String eventMessage;

    ...
}
```

And now, to fire the event. The simplest way to fire an event is with the trusty ol' BeanManager:

```
@Inject
BeanManager beanManager;

...

public void sendInterestingEvent(String message){
    InterestingEvent interestingEvent = new InterestingEvent();
    beanManager.fireEvent(interestingEvent,null);
}
```

What I've done here is shoot off an InterestingEvent into the CDI runtime. The event will be received by *observers* that have registered interest in InterestingEvents. What's that null bit? *You noticed!* I can optionally supply a list of CDI qualifiers (remember those?), to further narrow the list of candidate observers. How about an asynchronous event firing?

```
public void sendInterestingEvent(String message){

    ...

    CompletionStage completionStage = beanManager.getEvent().
    fireAsync(interestingEvent);
}
```

The async event firing gives you a standard JDK CompletionStage that I could optionally use to manage the threading or handle exceptions asynchronously. You've probably also noticed the inconsistency in the interface – if there's a fire method on BeanManager, there ought to be a fireAsync method also. Looking at you, JSR-365 expert group.[8]

Subscribe to CDI Events

With the event firing taken care of, now I just need to be paying attention with a CDI *Observer*:

```
public void listenForNews(@Observes InterestingEvent event (1))
{
        logger.info("Got some interesting news:
        "+event.getEventMessage();
}

public void listenForGossip(@Observes @Gossip InterestingEvent
event (2)){
        logger.info("Got some interesting gossip:
        "+event.getEventMessage();
}
```

---

[8]Editor's note: You could just open a pull request to contribute the change.

49

```
public void listenForGossipAsync(@ObservesAsync @Gossip
InterestingEvent event (3)){
        logger.info("Got some interesting gossip: "+event.
        getEventMessage();
}
```

1. Here I use @javax.enterprise.event.Observes to listen for events of the InterestingEvent type.

2. I'm interested in InterestingEvents only if they were fired with the @Gossip qualifier.

3. I can also listen asynchronously for @Gossip InterestingEvents.

So, bring your Spring beans in; let's give them the *Supersonic Subatomic* treatment!

CHAPTER 3

Microservices with Quarkus

Ahh yes, the raison d'etre of Quarkus: building microservices. We're not going to go through too much of the rudiments of microservices in Java. After going through this chapter however, you should gain an understanding of how to build a standards-based microservice using the Quarkus framework. If you're considering a migration of an existing service to Quarkus, you'll get an introduction to how to support some of the core microservice functionality, features, and configuration options you're probably already used to.

Note   While this chapter is titled for microservices, please don't take that as precluding vanilla web service implementations – "monoliths". Quarkus provides all the features you'll need in service-oriented architecture in general. Microservices are all the rage now, but spare a thought for the humble web service that's neither micro nor monolith. The Quarkus extension ecosystem will cover all your bases.

© Tayo Koleoso 2020
T. Koleoso, *Beginning Quarkus Framework*, https://doi.org/10.1007/978-1-4842-6032-6_3

Get Started with Microservices

I was going to title this section "How to Train Your Quarkus," but I had to pull that, because lawyers. If you use any of the available options for starting a Quarkus project, you're already on your way to writing a microservice. Like we saw earlier, you can get bootstrapped with the Quarkus starter at code.quarkus.io or a maven command:

```
mvn io.quarkus:quarkus-maven-plugin:1.5.0.Final:create
-DprojectGroupId=com.apress.samples -DprojectArtifactId=code-
with-quarkus -DprojectVersion=1.0.0-SNAPSHOT -DclassName=org.
acme.ExampleResource -Dpath=/hello
```

and you can start it in dev mode

```
mvn quarkus:dev
```

You can then hit your microservice with your preferred testing tool. I'm more of a Postman man myself, but there are many options. SoapUI is a darn fine alternative tool. You could also just hit the sample endpoint in a browser: `http://localhost:8080/hello`.

The **Java API for RESTful Web Services** or **JAX-RS** is the Java standard for building RESTful web services. It defines a standard set of annotations and classes that you use to implement RESTful or microservices in Java. The expectation is that software vendors then implement concrete libraries and frameworks based on the standard.

Quarkus supports the JAX-RS API by way of the **RESTEasy** library from Red Hat; you can expect to use almost all the functionality recommended by the JAX-RS specification and then some. You could also convert existing JAX-RS projects from other implementations like Jersey (from Oracle). This is the beauty of coding to standards: you can change the implementations of these standards, and your code can remain intact.

JAX-RS provides annotations, interfaces, and packaged components to handle all of the probable use cases you'll encounter while building microservices. We'll see some of the more advanced componentry as we saunter along this book, but for fundamental usage, you want to get to know

1. `@Path` to designate a class or a method as a web API endpoint

2. `@Consumes` and `@Produces` to designate what data formats (JSON, XML, etc.) a web API resource accepts and returns, respectively

3. The HTTP method annotations for handling different HTTP request types, from the `javax.ws.rs` package

   a. `@GET` for GET requests

   b. `@POST` for POST requests

   c. `@PUT` for PUT requests

   d. `@PATCH` for PATCH requests

   e. `@DELETE` for DELETE requests

   f. `@HEAD` for HEAD requests

4. The microservice request parameter handling annotations

   a. `@QueryParam` for accepting query parameters, for example, `http://yourservice.com/path/to/resource?someQueryParam=value`

   b. `@PathParam` for accepting parameters sent in web resource path, for example, `http://yourservice.com/path/parameters/here`

   c. `@MatrixParam` for processing fragments of parameters sent in the web resource path

    d. @FormParam for processing HTML form parameters

    e. @BeanParam for processing bean parameters

    f. @HeaderParam and @CookieParam for accepting parameters sent in the HTTP headers and cookies, respectively

The ExampleResource that was generated with the bootstrapping provides a small sample that you can get going immediately:

```
import javax.ws.rs.GET;
import javax.ws.rs.Path;
import javax.ws.rs.Produces;
import javax.ws.rs.core.MediaType;

@Path("/hello")(1)
public class ExampleResource {

    @GET (2)
    @Produces(MediaType.TEXT_PLAIN)(3)
    public String hello() {
        return "hello";
    }
}
```

What you get out of the box is an HTTP endpoint that allows a client to send an HTTP GET request and receive the simple "Hello" string as the response. JAX-RS can do a lot more. Here's what's going on here:

1. @Path defines the root URL "hello", at which the web service is available, relative to the deployment. Therefore, for a project on your personal computer named "code with quarkus", you can access this web service at http://localhost:8080/code-with-quarkus/hello.

2. @GET designates that this method can be accessed using an HTTP GET request method, making it a REST resource; you can access it via a browser URL load. It will not respond to any other HTTP method. Because this method doesn't carry its own @Path annotation, it's going default to the @Path annotation set at the class level.

3. @Produces defines the content type that this REST resource method will respond with. The MediaType enum contains all valid HTTP response types.

With the work saved, I can see my changes immediately, running in dev mode, as shown in Figure 3-1. I can now use a proper testing tool to try some of it out.

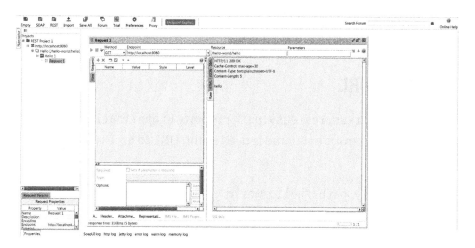

Figure 3-1. *The SoapUI interface for testing web services*

You can get SoapUI from www.soapui.org and Postman from www.getpostman.com. Both are very fine testing tools for web services.

Basic Microservice Configuration

According to the JAX-RS specification, you should subclass javax.ws.rs. core.Application and use that to configure your RESTful web service. Some of the basic configurations that would make javax.ws.rs.core. Application necessary have been simplified as configuration properties by Quarkus. All available Quarkus configurations are available and searchable at https://quarkus.io/guides/all-config; check it out!

Pro Tip   You can substitute OS-level properties into your Quarkus configuration file with the some.quarkus.property=${**<OS property>:<default-value>**} notation. This way, Quarkus will substitute the OS property value for that Quarkus property. Otherwise, it will use the default. Quarkus properties can also be overridden at the command line with -Dsome.quarkus.property=value.

Application URL

Configure the quarkus.resteasy.path property in application. properties to control what name is used in the URL to access the web service:

```
quarkus.resteasy.path=/hello-world
```

With that set, I can now access the microservice at http:// localhost:8080/hello-world/hello. The paths of the RESTful resource endpoint will still be controlled by the JAX-RS-annotated class, with @Path.

Application Name

Set the `quarkus.application.name` property to configure the name of the application. This affects the JAR artifact that's produced by Maven (or Gradle if that's your speed).

HTTP Server Port

Quarkus uses the Netty server: a lightweight workhorse of an app server with an adorable name and a can-do attitude. As with every other app server in enterprise Java, it defaults to port 8080 for deployed applications. Control that with `quarkus.http.port` and `quarkus.http.ssl-port` for HTTP and HTTPS endpoints, respectively.

TLS Settings

You can configure SSL certificates (or keystores if you're fancy) for use with the HTTPS port:

```
# The file path to a server certificate or certificate chain in
PEM format.
quarkus.http.ssl.certificate.file=<ssl-cert>
# The file path to the corresponding certificate private key
file in PEM format.
quarkus.http.ssl.certificate.key-file=<path>
# An optional key store which holds the certificate information
instead of specifying separate files.
quarkus.http.ssl.certificate.key-store-file=<keystore>
# An optional parameter to specify type of the key store file.
If not given, the type is automatically detected based on the
file name.
quarkus.http.ssl.certificate.key-store-file-type=JKS|PEM
```

```
# A parameter to specify the password of the key store file. If
not given, the default ("password") is used.
```
quarkus.http.ssl.certificate.key-store-password=<password>
```
# An optional trust store which holds the certificate
information of the certificates to trust
```
quarkus.http.ssl.certificate.trust-store-file=<file>
```
# A parameter to specify the password of the trust store file.
```
quarkus.http.ssl.certificate.trust-store-password=<password>

Application Host Address

Configure quarkus.http.host to set up the address at which you want to access your Quarkus microservice. This is a must-have for containerized applications – setting up quarkus.http.host=0.0.0.0 allows this microservice to listen on any network interface. Quarkus listens on 0.0.0.0 by default. *Container-friendly!*

Application Profiles

In Quarkus, you get one application.properties file to define your application configuration parameters – no environment-specific configuration file. Wait, wait; hear me out: you still get to define configurations for different deployment environments – profiles. Observe

%dev.quarkus.application.name=hello-goodbye
%aws-qa.quarkus.application.name=hello-aws-qa-goodbye

The %dev prefix in this sample marks that configuration property for the dev profile. Now, when I run my sample with java -jar /, only the dev profiled configs are loaded. So, between dev and some other profile, say aws-qa, my application can be named different things. This way, instead of having to (remember to) update multiple files with the same configuration parameter, you do it all in one place.

Quarkus provides three profiles out of the box:

- dev: What you get out of the box, with `quarkus:dev`

- test: What you get when running unit tests in Quarkus

- prod: What you get when you simply run `java -jar your-quarkus-project.jar`

You can start up in custom profiles by setting the `QUARKUS_PROFILE` OS-level parameter for the same results. For Windows, from a terminal window, set `QUARKUS_PROFILE = aws-qa`, and for *nix systems, export `QUARKUS_PROFILE = aws-qa`. With that, you can start up the quarkus app with

```
java -jar <quarkus jar name>-<version>-SNAPSHOT-runner.jar
```

You should see the correct profile displayed at startup:

```
INFO  [io.quarkus] (main) Profile aws-qa activated.
```

You can also configure the default startup profile with `quarkus. profile=<desired-profile>`.

Access Configuration Properties

Within the application itself, you have access to application properties with the `@ConfigProperty` annotation:

```
@Inject
@ConfigProperty(name="quarkus.application.name",defaultValue
="my-app-name" )
String applicationName;
```

This also loads the profile-specific version of the named configuration property. No, you can't have expression language (EL) in there like in your *precious* Spring Framework, for now. Properties can depend on each other with EL, however:

```
external.dependency.root = external.service.com
create.anagram.path = ${external.dependency.root}/create/
anagram
```

In this case, Quarkus will resolve the placeholder and build the correct path out for the dependent property.

Pro Tip   Microsoft Visual Studio Code will flag incorrect types supplied to properties file. For example, when I first tried out the `quarkus.log.console.color` config property, I set it as `quarkus.log.console.color=purple`. Because I can be daft at times and purple is my favorite color. MS VS Code highlighted it and showed me that that property is actually expecting a Boolean value. Now, not all consoles support colorization, so in Windows, for example, all you might see is the command-line equivalent of the markup that's supposed to effect the color change.

If you're interested in programmatically accessing configuration information:

```
String currentProfile = ProfileManager.getActiveProfile(); (1)
String appName = ConfigProvider.getConfig().getValue("quarkus.
application.name", String.class); (2)
```

What's going on here?

1. Use `ProfileManager.getActiveProfile()` to retrieve the currently active profile.

2. Use `ConfigProvider.getConfig().getValue()` to manually retrieve profile-bound application properties; you don't need to qualify the property names with the `%profile` prefix.

YAML Configuration Support

You can enable support for YAML format configuration by adding the YAML config extension:

```
mvn quarkus:add-extension -Dextension= quarkus-config-yaml
```

Service Content Types

Microservices should be RESTful by nature. That doesn't say anything about the message format that they should support. The sample REST resource that comes with the Quarkus starter responds with just a plain text "Hello" when you hit `http://localhost:8080/hello-world/hello` in a testing tool or in a browser (if you've configured the root path to be "hello-world").

For serious business, you need serious message formats like JSON or XML.[1] You can have JSON format support in Quarkus: use the JSON-B standard as prescribed by Jakarta/JavaEE; or use the Jackson library. As you already know, I'm a standards man, so JSON-B it is. I'll start by adding the JSON-B extension to my project:

```
mvn quarkus:add-extension -Dextension=quarkus-resteasy-jsonb
```

---

[1]Editor's note: …or Avro, Protobuf, etc. There are a lot of formats out there, man.

To further customize my JSON-B installation, I can supply an instance of JsonbConfigCustomizer like so:

```
import javax.json.bind.JsonbConfig;
import io.quarkus.jsonb.JsonbConfigCustomizer;

public class JSONConfig implements JsonbConfigCustomizer {
    public void customize(JsonbConfig config) {
        config.withNullValues(false);
    }
}
```

What I've done here is to define that null values should be ignored when processing incoming or outgoing REST payloads. Use the quarkus-resteasy-jaxb extension for XML support; use quarkus-jsonp for JSON-P support.[2]

Logging

There are JAX-RS specified ways to log. Then there are the simpler ways of Quarkus. Inside my application.properties file:

```
quarkus.log.console.format=%d{HH:mm:ss} %-5p [%c{2.}] (%t)
%s%e%n (1)
quarkus.log.console.level=FINEST (2)
quarkus.log.handler.console.enable = true|false (3)
```

With the preceding configurations

1. Configure the formatting of the log line. Quarkus provides a list of supported metacharacters that help you design your log output.

---

[2]JSON-P is a low-level JSON parsing API; JSON-B is a high-level functionality for JSON in Java. It's a little confusing since there's a JSONP standard in JavaScript land as well, and it doesn't have as much to do with JSON.

2. Configure the level of detail for the logs. The options
    are ALL,CONFIG,FINE,FINER,FINEST,OFF,SEVERE,
    WARNING.

3. Quarkus will log to the console by default; you can
    turn this off and send the log output directly to a file,
    to improve the throughput in logging.

If you'd like to get even fancier, you can configure the logging to be
async, which will yield even better throughput performance, at the risk of a
loss in fidelity depending on how it's configured:

```
quarkus.log.console.async=true (1)
quarkus.log.console.async.queue-length=1024 (2)
quarkus.log.handler.console.async.overflow=block|discard (3)
```

1. Enables asynchronous logging.

2. Sets the size of the buffer in memory, to which log
    content will be sent before being flushed to the
    console and visible.

3. Configures what to do when the in-memory buffer is
    full: block to disallow new content to be submitted
    to the buffer for logging; discard to...discard new
    log content after the buffer is full.

Asynchronous logging can yield overall big performance gains if
configured and tuned properly. There are other config items for Quarkus
logging; visit https://quarkus.io/guides/all-config to filter for more
logging-specific configurations.

JSON logging is also on the table, folks! You're going to enjoy JSON
logging in the cloud, particularly when integrated with log aggregators like
Splunk, Kibana, or even just AWS Cloudwatch. The structure of JSON is
readily digestible by both man and machine, and you know how we like
structure. Human beings too, I hear, like structure to some extent.

Add `quarkus-logging-json` extension to add support for JSON-formatted log output. Then you can configure JSON for your desired profile in application.properties:

```
%dev.quarkus.log.console.json=false
%test.quarkus.log.console.json=false
```

Omitting prod from this list leaves the logging in JSON format. Additionally, you can enable pretty printing with `quarkus.log.console.json.pretty-print=true`. Speaking of JSON...

Use JSON in Your REST Resource

So you've configured JSON for your microservice. How do you use it? I'm going to go back to my REST resource class and make the following changes:

```
@Path("/{name:[a-zA-Z]*}/scramble")(1)
@GET (2)
@Produces(MediaType.APPLICATION_JSON)(3)
public AnagramResponse getAnagram(@PathParam("name")(4)
final String nameToScramble){
    AnagramResponse response= generateAnagram(nameToScramble);
    return response;
}
@POST (5)
@Path("/scramble")
@Produces(MediaType.APPLICATION_JSON)
```

```
public AnagramResponse persistAnagram(AnagramRequest
anagramRequest){
    AnagramResponse response = generateAndSaveAnagram(anagr
    amRequest);
    return response;
}
```

OK, there's a little bit to unpack here, so stay with me:

1. I use the @Path annotation to configure the HTTP
    URL that I'll use to access this endpoint. In addition
    to just specifying the desired URL, I've also thrown
    in a bit of optional regex there - "[a-zA-Z]*". Why?
    Well, that expression acts as a validator. This REST
    endpoint will scramble the name supplied in the
    URL, and I've added validation to ensure that only
    alphanumeric names are supplied in the URL and
    that it's case-sensitive.

2. @GET makes sure that this method responds only to
    HTTP GET requests.

3. @Produces, together with MediaType.APPLICATION_
    JSON value, configures this REST resource to return
    JSON.

4. @PathParam picks up the text with the given
    placeholder title off the path (thanks to @Path).
    It then passes it into the method like a regular java
    method argument.

5. The persistAnagram resource does something
    like the getAnagram method. A difference here
    is that this method will respond only to HTTP
    POST requests sent to that URL. It accepts an

AnagramRequest request type and responds with
an AnagramResponse. The JSON-B in quarkus will
quietly serialize and deserialize the request and
response data objects, at no extra charge. This is
RESTEasy's doing.

Check out the RESTEasy documentation to see more annotations that
can help you handle request parameters and data efficiently and safely. All
these annotations are courtesy of the JAX-RS specification. Praise JAX-RS.

What's that? *More* JAX-RS? Well, if you insist.

JAX-RS Exception Handling

It happens to the best of us: an error or an exception occurs while your
application is trying to handle a request. It doesn't even have to be a bug,
could just be that bad input was supplied. It's tempting to pepper your
code with try-catch blocks and call it a day. The *boss* thing to do is to have
a focused component (or components) that will trap dedicated exception
types and respond appropriately. With the ExceptionMapper interface,
JAX-RS has you covered, friend:

```
import javax.ws.rs.core.Response;
import javax.ws.rs.ext.Provider;
import javax.ws.rs.ext.ExceptionMapper;

@Provider (1)
public class JAXRSExceptionMapper implements ExceptionMapper<Il
legalArgumentException> (2){
    final String EXCEPTION_MESSAGE = "invalid request data: ";
    final String RESPONSE_TYPE = "text/plain";
    @Override
```

```
public Response toResponse(IllegalArgumentException
exception(3)){
      return Response.serverError() .entity(EXCEPTION_
      MESSAGE+"exception.getMessage()") (4a)
.type(RESPONSE_TYPE) (4b)
.status(400)(4c)
.build();
   }
}
```

Okay then, come with me:

1. The class is annotated with @Provider to expose this class to the JAX-RS runtime as a framework enhancement.

2. I then implement the javax.ws.rs.ext. ExceptionMapper as stipulated by the JAX-RS specification. Together with the @Provider annotation, this class is then automatically registered with the runtime as the class that will handle all IllegalArgumentException thrown within the code of this web service.

3. The ExceptionMapper interface defines a single method, toResponse, which accepts the thrown exception as an argument.

4. I use the Response class builder to build the response I want – in this case, I

   a. Set the body of the response with the entity method

   b. Set the encoding type of the response

   c. Set the HTTP status of the response

No fuss, no muss. This class will be instantiated and used to process all `IllegalArgumentExceptions` generated inside this Quarkus application.

JAX-RS Filters and Interceptors

The JAX-RS specification defines filters and interceptors:

- **Filters**: To be able to modify parts of incoming requests or outgoing responses from your microservice. Within a filter, you have fine-grained access to the payloads in and out of your service; so you can transform the message or perform checks of the payload before or after they're handled by the resource methods.

- **Interceptors**: To repackage the entirety of the inbound or outbound messages of your microservice. This gives broad control over message payloads. Concerns like encryption and compression can be handled in here (Quarkus has out of the box compression configuration, so please don't roll your own).

Here they are in action.

Logging Filter

Yes, more logging – I'm going to position a filter in the processing chain, just to inspect and log the content of inbound and outbound messages in my REST service:

```
@Provider (1)
@Priority(1) (2)
public class LoggingFilter implements ContainerRequestFilter,
ContainerResponseFilter{
```

```
private final Logger logger = LoggerFactory.
getLogger(LoggingFilter.class.getName());

@Override
public void filter(ContainerRequestContext requestContext,
ContainerResponseContext responseContext)
        throws IOException {
            logger.info("Message on the way out
            "+responseContext.getEntity());

}

@Override
public void filter(ContainerRequestContext requestContext)
throws IOException {
    BufferedInputStream iStream = new BufferedInputStream(r
    equestContext.getEntityStream()); (3)
    byte[] inputContent = new byte[iStream.available()];
    iStream.read(inputContent);
    String body = new String(inputContent, "utf-8");
    logger.info("Inside request filter. Message size:
    "+inputContent.length+"; Message on the way in: "+body);
    requestContext.setEntityStream(new ByteArrayInputStream
    (inputContent));(4)

}
}
```

1. The @Provider annotation marks this class as a JAX-RS
   feature provider. Quarkus is contractually obligated to
   register this class and execute whatever JAX-RS feature
   it advertises. The @Priority annotation sets the priority
   of this filter relative to any other filters available.
   @Priority is provided by CDI.

2. The `ContainerRequestFilter` and
    `ContainerResponseFilter` interfaces define the
    contract for implementing inbound and outbound
    message filters, respectively. I've implemented both
    here so that I can use the same class to filter data in
    both directions to the microservice.

3. I get a hold of the inbound data so that I can do
    whatever I want with it.

4. I put the inbound data back where I found it. **This
    is important:** you must reset the inbound message
    stream; otherwise, the destination resource method
    will not see anything when processing gets to that
    point.

As you've probably deduced, JAX-RS filters are ideal for cross-cutting
concerns as well as command and control functionality. They're available
for both JAX-RS services and service clients. Want to route messages
elsewhere based on the request content? Do it in a filter. Want to stop a
message from ever getting to the targeted java method? Do it in a filter.
Want to perform authentication manually? Do. It. In. a. Filter.

Interceptors

Use interceptors when you want to act on the messages as a whole; unlike
filters that give you fine-grained access to the payloads, interceptors are for
the business of general manipulation of inbound and outbound messages:

```
import java.io.IOException;
import java.io.OutputStream;
import java.util.zip.GZIPOutputStream;
import java.util.zip.GZIPInputStream;
import javax.ws.rs.WebApplicationException;
```

```java
import javax.ws.rs.ext.ReaderInterceptor;
import javax.ws.rs.ext.ReaderInterceptorContext;
import javax.ws.rs.ext.WriterInterceptor;
import javax.ws.rs.ext.WriterInterceptorContext;
import javax.ws.rs.ext.Provider;

@Provider (1)
public class ReaderWriterInterceptor implements ReaderInterceptor,
WriterInterceptor (2){

        @Override
    public void aroundWriteTo(WriterInterceptorContext context)
    throws IOException, WebApplicationException {
        final OutputStream outputStream = context.
        getOutputStream();
        context.setOutputStream(encryptPayload(outputStream));
            context.proceed();
            }

            @Override
            public Object aroundReadFrom(ReaderInterc
            eptorContext context) throws IOException,
            WebApplicationException {
            final OutputStream inputStream = context.
            getInputStream();
            context.setInputStream(decryptPayload(inputStream));
            return context.proceed();

        }
    }
```

So what have we here?

1. @Provider again advertising to the Quarkus runtime that this is a JAX-RS component and that the CDI container had better take notice.

2. The ReaderInterceptor and WriterInterceptor interfaces. Use ReaderInterceptor for access to inbound messages to your web service; use WriterInterceptor for outbound messages.

3. In the ReaderInterceptor#aroundReadFrom method, I'm decrypting the entire inbound message payload.

4. In the WriterInterceptor's aroundWriteTo method, I'm encrypting the entire outbound message.

Both interceptor types have the power to halt the flow of messages, in or out, via their respective context objects. Speaking of *flow*...

Asynchronous RESTful Services in JAX-RS

JAX-RS (and Quarkus) operates REST services in synchronous mode by default: a client sends a request to connect; the embedded app server (Netty) uses a thread to serve the connection request. It uses that same thread to reach all the way into your microservice code, to execute the business logic that the client is requesting. Everything is brilliant, so long as the business logic doesn't take too long; "too long" is in the eye of the beer holder. The Netty app server is configured with a fixed size number of threads in a pool. With enough requests taking "too long," your microservice is going to go catatonic – the app server is going to run out of threads and throughput[3] nosedives.

The JAX-RS spec provides for asynchronous messaging from both the client and service perspectives. Async messaging allows the app server to execute business logic in a separate thread from the one that it uses to handle connection requests. This way, it can just receive an incoming service request in one thread and hand it off to a separate thread for actual business logic. That second thread is free to take as long as it needs to handle the business logic; the app server can quickly return its connection-handling thread back into the thread pool so it can serve more customers. There are a couple of ways to implement asynchronous messaging in JAX-RS. So what's going to happ-[4]

```
@Inject
ManagedExecutor managedExecutor; (1)

@GET
@Path("/{name:[a-zA-Z]*}/scramble-async ")
public void getAnagramAsync(@Suspended final AsyncResponse
async (2),final @PathParam("name")String name){
    final Future<?> toComplete  =  managedExecutor.
    submit(new Runnable() (3){
            @Override
            public void run() {
            logger.info("Executing in a different thread");
            final AnagramResponse response =
            getAnagram(name);
            async.resume(response) (4));

    });
}
```

---

[3]Throughput is a measure of how many concurrent requests or "customers" a service can handle at once.

[4]Editor's note: Enough talk! Show them the action!

```
@GET
@Path("/{name:[a-zA-Z]*}/scramble-rx")
public CompletionStage<AnagramResponse> getAnagramRx(final
@PathParam("name")String name){
    final CompletionStage<AnagramResponse>
    completionStageResponse = new CompletableFuture<>();
    managedExecutor.submit(new Runnable(){
            @Override
            public void run() {
            logger.info("Executing in different thread");
            final AnagramResponse response =
            getAnagram(name);
            ((CompletableFuture)completionStageResponse).
            complete(response);
        }

    });

    return completionStageResponse (3a);
}
```

1. I'm @Inject-ing a ManagedExecutorService; I installed the quarkus-smallrye-context-propagation Quarkus extension to support that. This is the safe way to multithread inside a Java web application. You will see a lot of examples online manually spinning up thread instances. Don't do that, it's not cool. The container will be able to manage threads a lot more efficiently than your custom code.

2. The @Suspended and AsyncResponse class are the special sauce here. When a method contains these two, it signals to the app container that "Hey, just

hand off the payload to the target method and return immediately. Don't wait for that method to return!". With that, all I need to do is

3. Submit a `Runnable` to the container's `ExecutorService`. **Remember**: Runnable is a JDK interface that defines the basic unit of work for a java thread to execute. Inside the runnable, I am delegating the actual operation to an existing resource method. Note that the return type of the suspended method is void. The response is going to go out on a different thread.

   a. An alternative approach to signaling to the runtime that this endpoint is an async endpoint is to return a `CompletionStage`. Feels more natural, I guess. The plumbing remains the same as for the `AsyncResponse` approach. A bonus is that with `CompletionStage` and `CompletableFuture`, you get a wholly reactive programming approach that allows you to specify exception handling scenarios among other things. Technically, this is a **reactive** approach to handling the requests, hence the "rx" name I have in "scramble-rx" (rx is the generally accepted shorthand for "Reactive").

4. I then send the result of the operation into the `resume` method of the `AsyncResponse` class, which then sends the response object back to the user on another thread. For the reactive approach, I needed to downcast the `CompletionStage` to a `CompletableFuture` and then call the complete method on that; it has the same effect as `AsyncResponse#resume`.

Now, this should be where everything ends: send a GET request to */hello/scramble-async* or */hello/scramble-rx*; the Netty thread hands the request over to a different thread and returns immediately. That second thread should then send the response object back via the AsyncResponse or CompletionStage. If I run this code as is, it'll fail – take it from me, I tried it first. For a couple of reasons, RESTEasy is no longer able to infer what the response type is supposed to be. To reinform the RESTEasy JAX-RS engine what the expected response type is, I need to use the generic Response class to wrap the return value.

Generic Response Wrapper in JAX-RS

I need to give Quarkus a hint as to what kind of response needs to be generated:

```
@GET
@Path("/{name:[a-zA-Z]*}/scramble-async")
@Produces(MediaType.APPLICATION_JSON)
public void getAnagramAsync(@Suspended final AsyncResponse
async,final @PathParam("name")String name){
    final Future<?> toComplete  =  managedExecutor.
submit(new Runnable(){
        @Override
        public void run() {
            logger.info("Executing in different thread");
            final Response response = Response.ok(getAnag
            ram(name)).type(MediaType.APPLICATION_JSON).
            build();
            async.resume(response);
            }
    });
    }
```

The javax.ws.rs.core.Response class is what you use as a generic, wrapper-type class for generating web service responses. Use it to build a response object on which you can set the HTTP status code, response type, and really anything that affects the output of the message. Using the response class to wrap the AnagramResponse object, I'm able to add the response type information as well as the desired HTTP status code. All's right with the world again.

Microservices, the RESTEasy Way

RESTEasy is Red Hat's implementation of the JAX-RS specification. It provides the features that the specification mandates and then enriches it with some pretty neat additional features. Quarkus' default REST API implementation is based on RESTEasy.

Cache Control

The core tenet of REST is to deal with service functionality using HTTP semantics. One of the things that HTTP defines is caching of responses from HTTP resources. org.jboss.resteasy.annotations.cache.Cache is a cheap way to introduce HTTP cache control semantics:

```
@GET
@Cache(maxAge = 30)
@Produces(MediaType.TEXT_PLAIN)
public String hello() {
...
}
```

This annotation lets you set different attributes that control how the various client-side cache control headers like max-age, no-store, and so on. Conversely, use @NoCache to disable setting these headers altogether.

Asynchronous Batch Processing in RESTEasy

This one's a very neat set of features, albeit neither not JAX-RS compliant. RESTEasy provides very cheap fire-and-forget service semantics. The RESTEasy platform can support asynchronous messaging without a lot of development effort. It's ideal for batch operations where the service client doesn't need an immediate response or even no response at all; and it's all supported by configuration alone with RESTEasy. So instead of all that typing we were doing per the JAX-RS standard, we could easily do the following.

Configure web.xml

Aye, Quarkus supports web.xml[5] too! web.xml support depends on Undertow, a web server.[6] So, I'll need to add the `quarkus-undertow` extension to my project. Following that, I can create and drop the following file into the META-INF directory of my project:

```
<web-app version="4.0"
    xmlns="http://xmlns.jcp.org/xml/ns/javaee"
    xmlns:xsi="http://www.w3.org/2001/XMLSchema-instance"
    xsi:schemaLocation="http://xmlns.jcp.org/xml/ns/javaee
    http://xmlns.jcp.org/xml/ns/javaee/web-app_4_0.xsd">

</web-app>
```

---

[5]This is the configuration file for web applications in JavaEE. It's as old as web programming in Java.

[6]Why is there an Undertow when Quarkus has Netty? They do different things: Netty is more concerned with the low-level plumbing involved in efficient network connection handling; Undertow *uses* Netty, but adds servlet support and a general web server layer on top of Netty.

Now for the meat of things. The following context parameters will bootstrap the RESTEasy async features:

```
<!-- How many batch jobs results can be held in memory at once? -->
    <context-param>
        <param-name>resteasy.async.job.service.max.job.
        results</param-name>
        <param-value>100</param-value>
    </context-param>

    <!-- Maximum wait time on a batch job when a client is
    querying for it -->
    <context-param>
        <param-name>resteasy.async.job.service.max.wait
        </param-name>
        <param-value>300000</param-value>
    </context-param>

    <!-- Thread pool size of background threads that run the
    batch job -->
    <context-param>
        <param-name>resteasy.async.job.service.thread.pool.
        size</param-name>
        <param-value>100</param-value>
    </context-param>

    <!-- Set the base path for the batch job uris -->
    <context-param>
        <param-name>resteasy.async.job.service.base.path
        </param-name>
        <param-value>/async/jobs</param-value>
    </context-param>
```

With this, I can now request an endpoint, say, */hello/Eyitayo/scramble?oneway=true*, and because of oneway=true, the response comes back immediately and the rest of the processing carries on on the server-side. Instead of responding with a payload, the service responds with HTTP-202, Accepted. This comes in very handy for kicking off batch processes. Read the RESTEasy guide on asynchronous batch jobs for more details on this feature.

Server-Side Caching

If you're looking to do more than just HTTP-based window dressing, Quarkus can cache the output from your microservice using io.quarkus.cache. CacheResult. Along with @CacheInvalidate and @CacheInvalidateAll, you can command and control the server-side cache. I'll add the cache extension and then I can do this:

```
@GET
@Path("/{name:[a-zA-Z]*}/scramble")
@Produces(MediaType.APPLICATION_JSON)
@CacheResult(cacheName="anagramCache")
public AnagramResponse getAnagram(@PathParam("name") final
String nameToScramble) {

        ...

}

 @CacheInvalidate(cacheName="anagramCache")
public void clearAnagramCache(String key){}

  @CacheInvalidateAll(cacheName="anagramCache")
public void clearAnagramCache(){}

@CacheInvalidateAll(cacheName="anagramCache")
@CacheInvalidateAll(cacheName="anagramSourceCache")
public void clearAllCaches(){}
```

@CacheResult will cache the response from a given method using Caffeine, a high performance cache provider. Quarkus will automatically create a cache named for cacheName; it uses a combination of the name of the method and the arguments supplied to it as the key.

When clearAnagramCache is invoked, it will clear the named cache, for the given key; you just need to compute the cache key correctly.

@CacheInvalidateAll will purge the cache named for cacheName when the annotated method is invoked. To control what constitutes the cache key, use @CacheKey:

```
@GET
@Path("/{name:[a-zA-Z]*}/scramble")
@Produces(MediaType.APPLICATION_JSON)
@CacheResult(cacheName="anagramCache")
public AnagramResponse getAnagram(@PathParam("name") @CacheKey
final String nameToScramble, long userId) {
    ...
}
```

With the preceding implementation, I'm selecting only the name passed in as a token for the cache key, intentionally excluding the other userId parameter.

Each available cache can be configured with named properties:

```
#minimum number of items to maintain in the cache
quarkus.cache.caffeine."anagramCache".initial-capacity=10
#maximum number of items to maintain in the cache. More than
this number, items will start being evicted automatically.
quarkus.cache.caffeine."anagramCache".maximum-size=20
```

Caffeine uses the Window-TinyLFU (W-TinyLfu) algorithm as its default cache eviction algorithm. It's been proven to be a near-optimal cache management algo, superior to the more popular Least Recently

Used (LRU) option. If for some reason you need to interrogate the caches directly, you can get a hold of them by obtaining the single instance of CacheRepository available:

```
@Inject
CacheRepository cacheRepository;
```

This grants you access to all the available caches in your Quarkus application. With that, you can programmatically manage your caches and their content.

Caution   Manually accessing the cache isn't an officially supported operation, so proceed with caution. Looking at the implementation of the CacheRepository class, it's not built with an interface, so the Quarkus team could break the implementation anytime.

Microservice Documentation with Swagger

I know, I know, writing documentation isn't sexy. But you know what else isn't sexy? Capri pants. Even less sexy: not knowing what an API does. That's where Swagger and the OpenAPI specification come in.

OpenAPI

OpenAPI defines a JSON or YAML-based structure for describing your web service to man and machine. You know how us machines like structure and predictability, right, fellow machine? Information such as the acceptable input types, expected output types, status codes, and so much more can be defined in a lightweight YAML (or JSON) document. Here's a small sample:

```
openapi: 3.0.1
info:
  title: Anagrams - The Quarkus Way
```

```
  description: This is an Anagram API. Send a string into one
  of the 'scramble' endpoints
    and it'll scramble the text
  contact:
    name: Tayo Koleoso
    url: http://www.apress.com
    email: tayo@somewhere.com
  license:
    name: Apache 2.0
    url: http://localhost:8080
  version: "0.0"
paths:
  /hello:
    get:
      summary: say hello
      description: says hello to you
      responses:
        "200":
          description: OK
          content:
            text/plain:
              schema:
                type: string
  /hello/hello-image:
    get:
      summary: Returns an image
      responses:
        "200":
          description: OK
```

This document has several benefits, chief among which is that it provides a consistent source of truth for man and machine. Based on what your web service exposes as its OpenAPI documentation, tools can be used to generate code based on the document; integration and testing tools can navigate your API intelligently. Also, humans can just read the document and know what's going on. I'll start by adding the SmallRye OpenAPI extension quarkus-smallrye-openapi to my project.

Next, I'm going to configure the URL at which I want the documentation to appear. Quarkus defaults it to the root of the web service, but I'm a bit of a control...enthusiast, so I'd like to change it. Also, this way, you can apply security constraints to that URL:

```
quarkus.smallrye-openapi.path=/docs/openapi
```

I can now visit ***http://localhost:8080/docs/openapi*** and get a download of the OpenAPI specification. This is all well and good, but what if I want is for people to be able to read this document and get human-readable information in it? For that, I'll turn to this suite of annotations that Swagger offers for defining OpenAPI output. Now, all the annotations don't just go anywhere. @OpenAPIDefinition is applicable to subclasses of javax.ws.rs.core.Application:

```
@OpenAPIDefinition (info =
    @Info(
                title = "Anagrams - The Quarkus Way",
                version = "0.1",
                description = "This is an Anagram API. Send a
                string into one of the 'scramble' endpoints and
                it'll scramble the text",
                license = @License(name = "Apache 2.0", url =
                "http://localhost:8080"),
                contact = @Contact(url = "http://www.apress.com",
                name = "Tayo", email = "tayo@somewhere.com")
```

```
    )
)
public class AppConfig extends Application{

}
```

Pro Tip   Your subclass of `javax.ws.rs.core.Application`
is where you have the most configuration control over your JAX-RS
microservice. Get to know it better!

For resource-specific OpenAPI documentation, we apply the Swagger
annotations on our REST methods:

```
@GET
@Path("/{name:[a-zA-Z]*}/scramble-async")
@Operation(summary = "scrambles the supplied username
asynchronously", description = "scrambles the name in the
path. There are no guarantees of uniqueness")
@APIResponses({@APIResponse(name = "Conversion
Response",responseCode = "200",description = "the scrambled
name. no uniqueness guarantees")})
public void getAnagramAsync(@Suspended final AsyncResponse
async,final @PathParam("name")String name){
    final Future<?> toComplete  =  managedExecutorService.
    submit(new Runnable(){
        @Override
        public void run() {
            logger.info("Executing in different thread");
            final Response response = Response.
            ok(getAnagram(name)).type(MediaType.
            APPLICATION_JSON).build();
```

```
                async.resume(response);
            }
        });
    }
```

So, when I open up `http://localhost:8080/hello-world/docs/`
`openapi`, I'll see all the information I've placed in OpenAPI annotations in
the code.

Swagger

Swagger, from the makers of SOAPUI, is an umbrella for a set of tools that
allow you to make the most out of OpenAPI. With the Swagger toolkit, we
can do sooo much more with our OpenAPI documentation. First check
out the Swagger UI (Figure 3-2) for your locally deployed Quarkus app at
`http://localhost:<port>/swagger-ui/`.

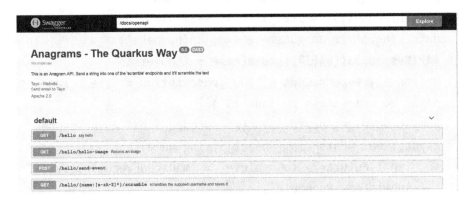

Figure 3-2. *The Swagger UI interface bundled with Quarkus*

Beautiful, isn't it? With the Swagger toolkit,

- You can generate code to interact with the REST service
  based on the OpenAPI spec.

- You can test an API using the Swagger UI, directly in the browser.

- You can modify the OpenAPI documentation live on the web service.

It's like the web service is carrying around its own portable testing and documentation kit. You can control where the Swagger UI shows up by setting `quarkus.swagger-ui.path` in the `application.properties` file; disable it altogether by setting `quarkus.swagger-ui.enable`. Check out the `Swagger website` for a deeper dive into its capabilities.

Fun Fact   Swagger was the first community-provided[7] extension for the Quarkus platform. Talk about a ringing endorsement!

MicroProfile Support

Eclipse MicroProfile is the cloud-native incarnation of Jakarta EE.[8] It's targeted at those looking to deploy "JavaEE" features in a cloud environment, but don't want the famous baggage that "JavaEE" brings with it. And when I titled this section "MicroProfile Support," it's a bit tongue-in-cheek as quite a lot of Quarkus is underpinned by MicroProfile. MicroProfile is a set of standards that are lightweight alternatives to anything you're already used to in the enterprise Java space (I refuse to type out JavaEE one more time. Dang it!). Some of the standards it offers are

- Configuration management

- Health checks

---

[7]`www.infoq.com/news/2019/04/redhat-quarkus-qa/`. Remember, Quarkus extensions are specially engineered to support the performance goals of the platform. This isn't just a matter of jamming a maven dependency in there.

[8]JavaEE is quickly becoming a dirty word.

- Fault tolerance

- Real-time performance metrics

- Distributed tracing

- Security

- OpenAPI support

- API client

As you may have guessed, the configuration management and OpenAPI functionality in Quarkus are directly provided by MicroProfile standard implementations. Let's check out some of its other standards.

REST Client

Are you tired of having to write a bunch of boilerplate code, every time your application needs to make a REST call to another service? The same old error handling, authentication logic. Every. Single. Time. No more! MicroProfile provides the REST client specification: minimal code, annotations for everything, and developer comfort are just some of the benefits of the MicroProfile REST client specification. Use the REST client to call other REST services from inside your Quarkus service. Simple enough, yeah? Think Spring Framework's `WebClient` and `RestTemplate` class rolled into one. The `quarkus-rest-client` extension supports the MicroProfile REST client in Quarkus, so in it goes:

```
mvn quarkus:add-extension -Dextension= quarkus-rest-client
```

Now, let me create a MicroProfile REST client. It starts and ends with an interface:

```
@RegisterRestClient(baseUri = "https://httpbin.org/")(1)
@RegisterProvider(LoggingFilter.class)(2)
```

```java
public interface HttpBinServiceDAO{
    @GET (3)
    @Path("/image/jpeg") (4)
    @Produces("image/jpeg")(5)
    CompletionStage<byte[]> (6) getImageAsync();

    @PATCH
    @Path("/delay/{delay}")
    @Produces(MediaType.APPLICATION_JSON)
    Response patchRandom(@PathParam("delay") int delay) throws
    Exception;

    @POST
    @Path("/anything/{anything}")
    @Produces(MediaType.APPLICATION_JSON)
    HttpBinAnythingResponse postAnything(
    @PathParam("anything")(6) String anything);

            }
```

Okay, stay with me here; there's a bit to unpack:

1. @RegisterRestClient advertises this interface as a
   rest client stub for MicroProfile/CDI to pick up. The
   baseURI configuration is the target REST resource's
   base address. With this annotation, I can later @Inject
   this interface wherever I need to connect to baseUri.
   Shout out to Kenneth Reitz, the proprietor of
   www.httpbin.org. Httpbin.org is an HTTP testing web
   service for *Requests* (Reitz's library), a python HTTP
   library. It allows devs to test their code against what's
   essentially a mock web service. So, you can copy-paste
   this code as is and it will have a service to talk to.

2. `@RegisterProvider` configures the supplied class as a JAX-RS provider for this client interface. **Remember:** I introduced providers in the JAX-RS section earlier; here I'm now registering a `LoggingFilter` as a provider.

3. `@GET` defines this method for executing a GET request against the defined `@Path`. Remember, this will be appended to the `baseURI`, so that the final request URI in this example will read as `https://httpbin.org/image/jpeg`.

4. `@Produces` defines the expected response type from the target endpoint.

5. The `CompletionStage` return type signals to the application runtime that this request is a reactive one. I use it here to wrap the binary data in the response from `httpbin.org`, for that specific endpoint. Flagging this as reactive makes this request asynchronous, event-driven, and CPU-efficient. The best of three worlds.

6. `@PathParam` here will take the argument to that method and patch it into the right position in the `@Path`.

All that done, how do we use any of it? CDI, baby!

```
@Inject
@RestClient (1)
HttpBinServiceDAO httpBinService;

    @GET
    @Path("/hello-image")
    @Cache(maxAge = 30)
```

```
@Operation(summary = "Returns an image")
@Produces("image/jpg")
public Response helloImage() throws InterruptedException,
ExecutionException {
    CompletionStage<byte[]> futureImage = httpBinService.
    getImageAsync() (2);
    byte[] imageBytes = futureImage.toCompletableFuture().
    get()(3);
    return Response.ok().entity(new StreamingOutput(){ (4)
        @Override
        public void write(OutputStream output)
            throws IOException, WebApplicationException {
            output.write(imageBytes);
            output.flush();
        }
    }).build()(5);
}
```

Here we go again. Hang on to your hoodies, nerds:

1. I inject the REST client interface and mark it with
   the @RestClient annotation. Again, MicroProfile
   REST clients are available in any part of the Quarkus
   application; it doesn't have to be inside of a JAX-RS
   resource class.

2. In the helloImage method, I execute the
   getImageAsync operation on the rest client. The
   method returns a CompletionStage, because it's a
   reactive method. At this point, we're back in vanilla
   Java/JAX-RS. We're done with any special Quarkus
   or MicroProfile business.

91

3. I convert the `CompletionStage` to a `CompletableFuture`; this is to make it simple to retrieve the response object. Note that the use of `CompletionStage` is to provide reactive java support.

4. I use the generic `Response` object (remember that thing from back then?) to construct a HTTP response fit to carry an image. This is supported purely with the JAX-RS standard. Simply pass an instance of `StreamingOutput` to the `entity` method of `Response`.

5. Finally, I call the `build` method to construct the actual response object.

So I can go to the browser and request `http://localhost:8080/hello/hello-image` and it will go out to `www.httpbin.org` and fetch an image to display in my browser. Feel free to use your preferred testing tool to try out the other endpoints. You can control a fair bit of the client with configuration properties.

Client Exception Handling

Look, I don't know about you, but my code's perfect – never fails. Never. Now in case *you* need to handle exceptions in your MicroProfile rest client, create a `ResponseExceptionMapper`:

```
import javax.ws.rs.core.Response;
import javax.ws.rs.ext.Provider;
import org.eclipse.microprofile.rest.client.ext.
ResponseExceptionMapper;
```

```
@Provider
public class HttpBinExceptionMapper  implements ResponseExcepti
onMapper<ErrorMessage>{
    @Override
    public ExecutionException toThrowable(Response response) {
        // do something with the content of the response and
        rethrow the exception
            String errorMessage = response.readEntity(String.
            class);
        return new Exception(errorMessage);
    }
}
```

Then register the ResponseExceptionMapper on the rest client interface:

```
@RegisterProvider(LoggingFilter.class)
@RegisterProvider(HttpBinExceptionMapper.class)
@RegisterRestClient(baseUri = "https://httpbin.org/")
public interface HttpBinServiceDAO{
...
}
```

The exception mapper will be triggered only if an HTTP status code of 400 or greater is returned by the service call. You can also skip this manual registration entirely, adding @Provider to the exception handling class itself; it'll be picked automatically by the RESTEasy runtime. This class is then able to take the failure response from the REST service – say an HTTP 403 response – and map it to an exception type you're prepared to handle. Sort of the inverse of the JAX-RS ExceptionMapper that maps exceptions to Response objects. Note that by default, the MicroProfile REST client will map all failures to javax.ws.rs.WebApplicationException.

Authentication

For some reason, some REST resources require authentication and authorization. *shrug*. Obviously, if the auth credentials are expected in the URL or request body, those are easy to add. For the header-based authentication and really, any client headers that need to go out with the request, use @ClientHeaderParam (or @ClientHeaderParams to add multiple client headers at once):

```
@RegisterProvider(LoggingFilter.class)
@RegisterProvider(HttpBinExceptionMapper.class)
@RegisterRestClient(baseUri = "https://httpbin.org/")
@ClientHeaderParam(name="Authorization",value =
"{computeBasicAuthHeader}")(1)
public interface HttpBinServiceDAO{

...

default String computeBasicAuthHeader(){ (2)
        LOGGER.info("Computing basic auth header ");
        return "Basic " + Base64.getEncoder().encodeToString(
        "username:password".getBytes());

    }
}
```

Here's what's happening:

1. I've defined the @ClientHeaderParam for the HTTP Basic authorization header. The value attribute can be hard-coded, but in my case, I'm delegating it to a custom method named computeBasicAuthHeader.

2. The implementation of computeBasicAuthHeader as a default method.

For any invocation of this MicroProfile rest client, computeBasicAuthHeader will be executed to supply the value for that header. I have the option of applying the @ClientHeaderParam annotation to the individual methods in this REST client interface as well; each method will have individual header computations. I'm also allowed to obtain configured credentials using the MicroProfile config API, so you don't have to hard-code anything. I can also refer to classes outside of the interface – value="{org.acme.headers.HeaderFactory}" will load header values generated by the hypothetical HeaderFactory class.

For even greater control over the rest client, you can do away with the annotations and use a org.eclipse.microprofile.rest.client. RestClientBuilder to manually construct and utilize the REST client:

```
HttpBinServiceDAO binServiceDao = RestClientBuilder.
newBuilder()
            .baseUrl(new URL("http://httpbin.org/"))
            .build(HttpBinServiceDAO.class);
```

With this setup, you can configure

- Connection timeouts

- Providers

- Interceptors

- Filters

- SSL parameters

- JAX-RS feature classes

Truly powerful stuff.

Configure Client SSL

Again with this security business? Fine, if your target REST service is SSL-secured, you can comply by configuring a custom Java Key Store (JKS) file and the following configuration parameters. The values can be found either by directly referencing the file with `file://` or anywhere in the classpath with `classpath:/`

```
#set the trust store location.
org.acme.rest.HttpBinDAO/mp-rest/trustStore =
[classpath|file]:/client-truststore.jks
#set the trust store password
org.acme.rest.HttpBinDAO/mp-rest/trustStorePassword =password
#set the key store location
org.acme.rest.HttpBinDAO/mp-rest/keyStore = [classpath |
file]:/client-keystore.jks
#set the keystore password
org.acme.rest.HttpBinDAO /mp-rest/keyStorePassword = password
#set the keystore type. JKS is the default
org.acme.rest.HttpBinDAO/mp-rest/keyStoreType=PEM
```

The configuration scheme here is an acquired taste. You use the fully qualified class name (FQCN) – `org.acme.rest.HttpBinDAO` in this case – as the base for the property. Then you follow it up with `/mp-rest/` and then the specific property you'd like to configure.

While we're on the subject of security…

Security

First, let's get the obvious out of the way: this is a Java-based platform that supports the well-known *web.xml*, so you have access to "legacy" security mechanisms that *web.xml* offers. We're here for newer, shinier stuff.

CORS

Cross-origin resource sharing (CORS) is fancy HTTP-speak for "as a web service or resource, I will allow only requests from the same web domain as me to request data from me. Requests from a different domain will be bounced. Unless that different domain is on a shortlist I maintain".
This is typically enforced by a browser: a web page running on www.yourwebapplication.com will not be allowed to request resources from http://asubdomain.yourwebapplication.com. Unless it has been specifically allowed by yourwebapplication.com via CORS HTTP headers, the requests will be disallowed. It gets super specific too: you can filter requests by HTTP method, allowed headers, and allowed origins (i.e., what domains are even allowed to make CORS requests to yourwebapplication.com).

Lesser frameworks might make you write your own filter to modify an HTTP request to allow CORS. Quarkus makes it easy; here are the configuration parameters to get that sorted out:

```
# Enable the CORS filter.
quarkus.http.cors=true

# HTTP headers exposed in CORS
# Comma separated list of valid headers. ex: X-Custom,Content-
#Disposition
quarkus.http.cors.exposed-headers=Content-Disposition

# HTTP methods allowed for CORS
# Comma separated list of valid methods. ex: GET,PUT,POST
# The filter allows any method if this is not set.
# default: returns any requested method as valid
quarkus.http.cors.methods=GET,PUT,PATCH,POST
```

```
# Origins allowed for CORS
# Comma separated list of valid URLs. ex:
#http://www.quarkus.io,http://localhost:3000
# The filter allows any origin if this is not set.
# default: returns any requested origin as valid
quarkus.http.cors.origins=asubdomain.yourwebapplication.com
```

Role-Based Authentication and Authorization

Quarkus delegates security to different extensions, based on how they work:

- OpenID

- JSON Web Token (JWT)

- Property file

- JDBC

- Keycloak

- Built-in security mechanisms:

    - FORM

    - HTTP-BASIC

    - DIGEST

    - CLIENT-CERT

The built-in authentication mechanisms are easy enough to configure using just properties. For development purposes, for example, quarkus-elytron-security-properties-file allows you to configure user credentials in your application.properties. To use industrial strength authentication, you'll need to go for adult authentication options like JWT, SQL, or frameworks like OAuth and OpenID.

I'll decide which authorization mechanism to demonstrate by the end of this senten- I have decided: I will now demonstrate the JWT support in MicroProfile.

JSON Web Tokens

The JSON Web Token (JWT) standard is an open source authentication and authorization standard; it looks to provide those two services in a distributed computing ecosystem (read: the Internet). It's an industry standard that provides signed and/or encrypted JSON objects, to be used as credential tokens. I show a typical flow of a service-to-service authentication that uses JWT in Figure 3-3.

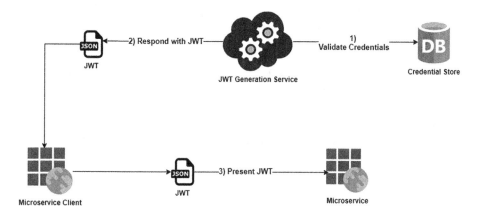

Figure 3-3. *A basic JWT authentication flow*

Here's how it works:

1. A subject (web service client, other service) will authenticate against a JWT provider with regular credentials like username/password.

2. The JWT provider will generate and issue a JWT to an approved requester. Each JWT contains what is known as claims. A claim is a piece of information

that can be used to correctly validate the authenticity of entity that is presenting that claim. So, "assume" that I, Tayo, am a web service client machine. If I'm requesting a JWT, one of the claims in that JWT could be "name: Tayo".

3.   The service client will then continue to present the issued JWT to the service for every request; if that JWT was signed or encrypted using the right keys recognized by the service, the service client's request will be honored. So instead of re-presenting the username/password every time, the client presents the token.

JWTs can be signed, encrypted, validated, and revoked on schedule, making them quite versatile. There are industry standard claim fields that have been defined by the JWT governing body, but you're free to define your own. JWTs can also be used with other security protocols like OpenID and OAuth. Read more about the JWT standard here.[9]

The MicroProfile specification has minimum security requirements for using JWT: as at the time of this writing, JWTs must be signed with the RSASSA-PKCS-v1_5, using the SHA256 algorithm with 2048-bit key strength; there are other JWT implementations, and they might not be so exacting. To demonstrate this will be in two stages.

Generate a JWT

Ideally, a central service or component in your architecture will be responsible for generating a JWT. For this demonstration, I'll just provide

---

[9]Also check out my LinkedIn Learning video where I do a step-by-step walk-through of generating and validating a JWT in a Jersey application.

a REST endpoint that generates a JWT, using the first and last names of the requester as claims to add to the JWT:@**Path("/")**:

```
public class JWTIssuerResource{

    final Logger logger = LoggerFactory.
    getLogger(JWTIssuerResource.class.getName());

    @GET
    @Produces(MediaType.TEXT_PLAIN)
    @Path("/{firstName}/{lastName}/generate-token-for")
    public Response getJWT(@PathParam("firstName")String
    firstName, @PathParam("lastName")String lastName){
        String jwt= generateAndSignJWT(...);
        return Response.ok(jwt).build();
    }
}
```

Okay, so the generator endpoint skeleton is in place. I'll take you on a magic carpet ride of what the generateAndSignJWT method looks like. So that I can sign and encrypt the JWT, I need a set of encryption keys. I'll use OpenSSL to generate keys. I'm downloading the OpenSSL utility for my OS from (just web search "Openssl for <your OS>").

After getting my OpenSSL unpacked onto my machine, I add the unpacked download to my OS's path, so that I can execute the tools from any location. Then I open up a terminal window to

1. Generate a base key with the following command: openssl genrsa -out baseKey.pem 2048. The base key that is generated is a .pem file in the current folder.

2. Generate a PKCS#8 private key: openssl pkcs8 -topk8 -inform PEM -in baseKey.pem -out privateKey.pem -nocrypt. This is what I'll sign and encrypt the JWT with.

3. Generate a public key: `openssl rsa -in baseKey.`
    `pem -pubout -outform PEM -out publicKey.pem`.

I'll stash the private key in resources directory of my Quarkus app – do this more securely in a production application; the public key goes in the META-INF directory. Next, there's some configurin' to do. First, I'll add the smallrye-jwt extension; then I'll need to configure the key and my issuer name:

```
mp.jwt.verify.publickey.location=META-INF/resources/publicKey.pem
mp.jwt.verify.issuer = SupersonicSubatomic
```

These are prerequisite configs per the MicroProfile specification.

All done with configuration, I start codin', first with loading the private key:

```
PrivateKey loadPrivateKey() throws IOException,
InvalidKeySpecException, NoSuchAlgorithmException{
        //load the raw file
        byte[] keyFileBuffer = CustomJWTIssuerResource.class.
        getResourceAsStream("/META-INF/privateKey.pem").
        readAllBytes();

        //strip marker text from the raw key text
        String cleanKey = new String(keyFileBuffer, 0,
        keyFileBuffer.length).replaceAll("-----BEGIN (.*)-----
        ", "")
                                .replaceAll("-----END (.*)----", "")
                                .replaceAll("\r\n", "")
                                .replaceAll("\n", "")
                                .trim();
        //convert text to PKCS8/RSA key
```

```
    return KeyFactory.getInstance("RSA").
    generatePrivate(new PKCS8EncodedKeySpec(Base64.
    getDecoder().decode(cleanKey)));
}
```

Then I use the key

```
String generateAndSignJWT(String firstName,
String lastName,List groups, Map roles) throws
InvalidKeySpecException, NoSuchAlgorithmException, IOException{
    Map<String,Object> claimsMap = new HashMap<>();
    claimsMap.put("firstName", firstName);
    claimsMap.put("lastName", lastName);
    JwtClaimsBuilder claims = Jwt.claims(claimsMap)(1)
                                    .subject(firstName+"
                                    "+lastName)
                                    .claim("roleMappings", roles)
                                    .claim("groups", groups)
                                    .issuer(jwtIssuer)
                                    .issuedAt(Instant.now().
                                    toEpochMilli())
                                    .expiresAt(Instant.now().
                                    plus(2, ChronoUnit.DAYS).
                                    toEpochMilli());
    PrivateKey privateKey = loadPrivateKey();
    return claims.jws().sign(privateKey); (2)
}
```

1. I start by generating a JWT object using the JWTBuilder class. I bulk-add the first and last names as custom claims, along with other claims. The "groups" and "roles" claims must be set for role-based authentication (RBAC) to work.

2. I then use the key to sign the generated JWT. At this point, the JWT has been transformed into a string. Here's the complete operation as a REST resource:

```
Path("/")
public class JWTIssuerResource{

    @Inject
    @ConfigProperty(name="mp.jwt.verify.issuer",defaultValue
    ="my-issuer-name" )
    String jwtIssuer;

    final Logger logger = LoggerFactory.
    getLogger(JWTIssuerResource.class.getName());


@GET
@Produces(MediaType.TEXT_PLAIN)
@Path("/{firstName}/{lastName}/generate-token-for")
public Response getJWT(@PathParam("firstName")String firstName,
@PathParam("lastName")String lastName){
        String JWT = null;
            try {
            Map<String,Object> rolesMap = new HashMap<>();
            rolesMap.put("role 1","VIP");
            rolesMap.put("role 2","VVIP");
            rolesMap.put("role 3","visitor");
            List<String> groups = new ArrayList<>();
            groups.add("Group 1");
```

```
        JWT = generateAndSignJWT(firstName,
        lastName,groups,rolesMap);
        } catch (InvalidKeySpecException |
        NoSuchAlgorithmException | IOException e) {
            // TODO Auto-generated catch block
            e.printStackTrace();
        }
    return Response.ok(JWT).build();
}

public String generateAndSignJWT(String firstName,
String lastName,List groups, Map roles) throws
InvalidKeySpecException, NoSuchAlgorithmException, IOException{
        Map<String,Object> claimsMap = new HashMap<>();
        claimsMap.put("firstName", firstName);
        claimsMap.put("lastName", lastName);
        JwtClaimsBuilder claims = Jwt.claims(claimsMap)
                                    .subject(firstName+"
                                    "+lastName)
                                    .claim("roleMappings",
                                    roles)
                                    .claim("groups", groups)
                                    .issuer(jwtIssuer)
                                    .issuedAt(Instant.now().
                                    toEpochMilli())
                                    .expiresAt(Instant.now().
                                    plus(2, ChronoUnit.DAYS).
                                    toEpochMilli());
        PrivateKey privateKey = loadPrivateKey();
        return claims.jws().sign(privateKey);

}
```

```
PrivateKey loadPrivateKey() throws IOException,
InvalidKeySpecException, NoSuchAlgorithmException{
    //load the raw file
    byte[] keyFileBuffer = JWTIssuerResource.class.
    getResourceAsStream("/META-INF/privateKey.pem").
    readAllBytes();

    //strip marker text from the raw text
    String cleanKey = new String(keyFileBuffer, 0,
    keyFileBuffer.length).replaceAll("-----BEGIN (.*)-----
    ", "")
                            .replaceAll("-----END (.*)----", "")
                            .replaceAll("\r\n", "")
                            .replaceAll("\n", "")
                            .trim();
    //convert text to PKCS8/RSA key
    return KeyFactory.getInstance("RSA").
    generatePrivate(new PKCS8EncodedKeySpec(Base64.
    getDecoder().decode(cleanKey)));
    }
}
```

So, when I navigate to http://localhost:8080/hello/generate-jwt,
I'll see the Base64-encoded JWT in the browser; to verify it's legit, paste the
text into the debugger over at www.jwt.io. You should see the claims in the
box on the right side.

This is a rough approximation of the process of generating a token by
a proper token vendor in an enterprise architecture – the vendor could be
the microservice itself or a central system like Keycloak; architecturally,
it works best when a dedicated system vends the JWT token to service
clients. The token should be presented by the holder every time it needs
access to a protected resource – this resource just needs to use the private
key to verify that the token is legit.

Server-Side JWT-Protected Access

Let's now see how you can use JWTs to protect access to your microservice. It starts with the @RolesAllowed annotation. The @RolesAllowed annotation is from the Jakarta EE specification for security; this isn't a Quarkus or JAX-RS supplied component:

```
@GET
@Path("/{name:[a-zA-Z]*}/scramble-async")
@RolesAllowed("VIP")
@Operation(summary = "scrambles the supplied name
asynchronously", description = "scrambles the name in the
path. There are no guarantees of uniqueness")
...
public void getAnagramAsync(@Suspended final AsyncResponse
async,final @PathParam("name")String name){
    ...
}
```

Having added @RolesAllowed("VIP") to that resource method, I'm allowing only JWT claims with "VIP" in the role claim to access that resource; therefore, it's crucial that the role be set as a claim on the JWT. The issuer claim also must match what's configured for **mp.jwt. verify.issuer** in the application.properties file:

```
mp.jwt.verify.issuer = SupersonicSubatomic
```

Next, I'll slap the @LoginConfig annotation on the javax.ws.rs.core. Application class to enable JWT protected access:

```
@LoginConfig(authMethod = "MP-JWT",realmName = "TCK-MP-JWT")
@OpenAPIDefinition (info =
    @Info(title = "Anagrams - The Quarkus Way",
                version = "0.0",
```

```
                    description = "This is an Anagram API. Send a
                    string into one of the 'scramble' endpoints and
                    it'll scramble the text",
                    license = @License(name = "Apache 2.0", url =
                    "http://localhost:8080"),
                    contact = @Contact(url = "http://www.apress.com",
                    name = "Tayo", email = "tayo@somewhere.com")
        )
)
public class AppConfig extends Application{

}
```

The authMethod and realmName values are prescribed by MicroProfile – they must be MP-JWT and TCK-MP-JWT, respectively. Now I should be able to hit that endpoint with SoapUI. The JWT token is set in the Authorization header as I demonstrate in Figure 3-4:

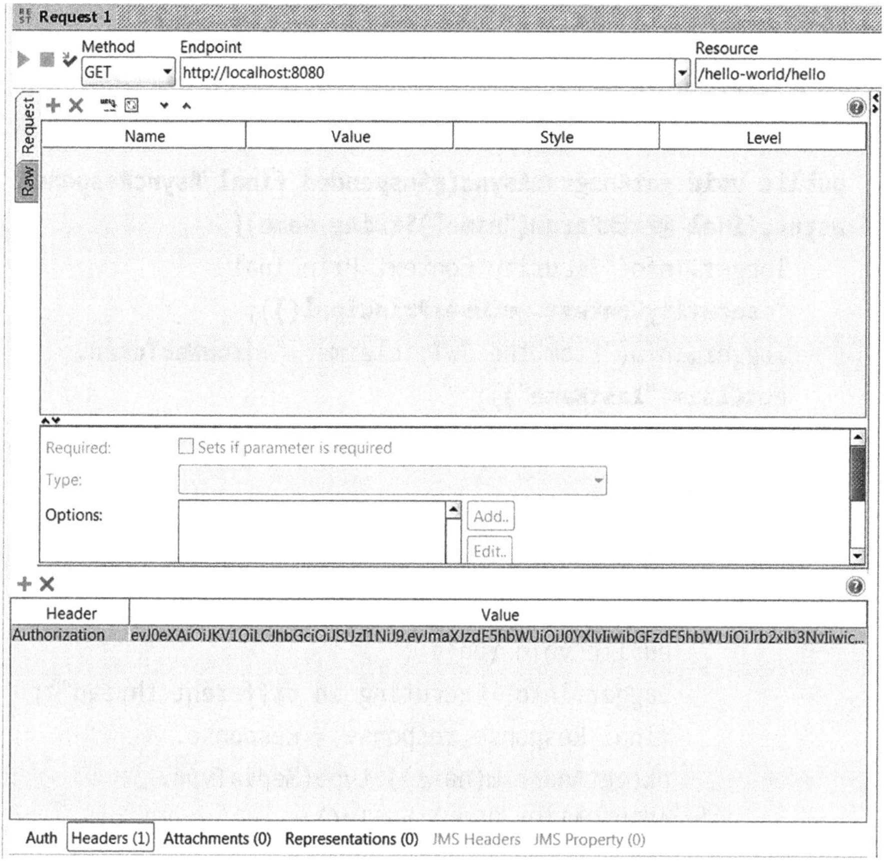

Figure 3-4. *Sending the Base64-encoded JWT in the Authorization HTTP header*

Now that the request can be authorized to fulfillment, I can use the SecurityContext and JsonWebToken objects to get more information about the requesting client:

```
@Context
SecurityContext securityContext;

@Inject
JsonWebToken jsonWebToken;
```

```
@GET
@Path("/{name:[a-zA-Z]*}/scramble-async")
@RolesAllowed("VIP")
...
public void getAnagramAsync(@Suspended final AsyncResponse
async,final @PathParam("name")String name){
    logger.info("Security Context Principal
    "+securityContext.getUserPrincipal());
    logger.info("From the JWT, claims: "+jsonWebToken.
    getClaim("lastName"));
    logger.info("From the JWT, subject: "+jsonWebToken.
    getSubject());
    final Future<?> toComplete  =  managedExecutorService.
    submit(new Runnable(){
            @Override
            public void run() {
            logger.info("Executing in different thread");
            final Response response = Response.
            ok(getAnagram(name)).type(MediaType.
            APPLICATION_JSON).build();
            async.resume(response);
        }
    });
}
```

The JsonWebToken object is provided by MicroProfile to access the JWT object; the SecurityContext object is a JAX-RS component that allows you to interrogate the platform for information about authenticated parties.

And that, team, is how I implement JWT role-based access (RBAC) security in MicroProfile, by way of Quarkus. This is largely just an authorization check. For authentication, consider combining this with a credential check inside of a ContainerRequestFilter.

Ideally, you shouldn't have to write a lot of this kind of authentication and authorization by yourself. Consider using a canned service like KeyCloak together with OAuth, to provide centralized management and validation of your tokens and other security bits and bobs; Quarkus provides both OAuth and Keycloak extensions. You only need to install the extensions, configure and manage your authentication and authorization in Keycloak.

Configuration

I've been configuring in a couple of demonstrations so far, so hopefully you're not a stranger to code like this:

```
@Inject
@ConfigProperty(name="my.property",defaultValue ="default-
value" )
String myProperty;
```

There's a little more to configuration in Quarkus. Quarkus' configuration is supported by MicroProfile (like a bunch of other things in Quarkus). So, in addition to the vanilla stuff, I can have

```
@Inject
@ConfigProperty(name="my.app.dynamic-property",defaultValue
="my-dynamic-ppty" )
Provider<String> myDynamicProperty;
...
public void readProperty(){
    logger.info("Current property value: "+ myDynamicProperty.
    get());
}
```

This approach will supply live values every time it's looked up with the get() method; it's a lazy-loading approach. In a cloud setting, with a centrally managed configuration system (maybe Spring cloud or even a flat file somewhere), you can modify configurations and have the changes take effect in a deployed application.

I can collect configuration items into collections like so:

```
my.app.list.of.admins=tayo,keni,kitti,eden
```

And in the code, that comma-separated list of configurations will be collected into a collection:

```
@Inject
@ConfigProperty(name="my.app.list.of.admins")
Set<String> admins;
```

Matter of fact, Quarkus allows me to dispense with @Inject altogether:

```
@ConfigProperty(name="my.app.list.of.admins")
Set<String> admins;
```

Personally, I'm not a fan of skipping annotations, because it breaks the CDI specification. Keeping with the specification ensures that everyone reading the same code can immediately come to the same understanding, without needing someone to explain quirks of a specific platform to them. Or maybe I'm just an old man who isn't as hip as he thought.

Health Checks

You're not going to have a good time cloud deploying a microservice if you're not providing a health check endpoint. Think of the health check endpoint as a way for anyone or anything to confirm that your service hasn't died and gone to microservice heaven. Successful container-based application deployment and management (using Swarm or Kubernetes) relies on being able to confirm the state of a microservice, with health checks. Then when you're talking about the cloud, services like the Elastic Container Service (ECS) and Elastic Kubernetes Service (EKS) need health checks for deployment. The MicroProfile Health Check specification defines two categories of health checks:

- **Liveness**: Use @Liveness check to indicate whether the service is **live**, able to accept requests or not. In a scenario where the service is down and is in the process of starting up or healing from a failure, this check should fail. The result of this check is available by default at <approot>/health/live.

- **Readiness**: This check is made available at <approot>/health/ready. Use @Readiness to verify that the service is ready. A service could be running, that is, still active in the Java process, but might not be in a state to serve requests. For example, a file storage service that has run out of disk space: sure it's up and running, but is it **ready**? *Nyet.*

I'll add the SmallRye Health extension to the project:

```
mvn quarkus:add-extension -Dextension=quarkus-smallrye-health
```

One way of implementing these health check annotations is to decorate a CDI bean's methods:

```
...
import org.eclipse.microprofile.health.HealthCheck;
import org.eclipse.microprofile.health.HealthCheckResponse;
import org.eclipse.microprofile.health.Readiness;

...
```

```
@ApplicationScoped (1)
public class HealthCheckProvider{

    @Produces (2)
    @Readiness (3)
    @Named("diskSpaceHealth")
    HealthCheck (5) getChecked(){
        return new HealthCheck() {
            @Override
            public HealthCheckResponse call() {
                return HealthCheckResponse.named
                ("diskSpaceCheck").state
                (isDiskSpaceAvailable()).withData
                ("arbitraryVariable", "arbitraryValue").
                build();
            }
        };
    }

    boolean isDiskSpaceAvailable(){
        //dummy implementation, obviously
        return Boolean.TRUE;
    }
}
```

1. A CDI bean scoped with @ApplicationScoped
   means there's only one instance of it available in the
   entire application. This makes sense from a design
   perspective – you should have only one source of
   truth in your entire application.

2. @Produces designates this method as a producer of
   health check data.

3. `@Readiness` designates this method as producing Readiness information.

4. `@Named` gives a custom name to this health check. This is a matter of best practice, to help forestall any ambiguity with other health check endpoints you might introduce into your application.

5. I return an instance of `HealthCheck`, based on the return value of a disk space checking method. I also get to add arbitrary data and name the health check itself.

The CDI runtime will automatically pick up this health check producer and make it available **at** `http://localhost:8080/health/ready`. I'll then see the status "UP" or "DOWN" depending on the result of the check. I'll also find the data I chose to publish. Figure 3-5 shows what the ready endpoint page looks like:

Figure 3-5. *The response generated by the ready endpoint*

To be clear, this isn't the only way to implement health checks with MicroProfile. I recommend this because it allows me to cleanly inject the health check anywhere else in my Quarkus app:

```
@Inject
@Readiness
HealthCheck diskCheck;
```

```
...
void getDiskReadiness(){
logger.info("Disk check status:"+ diskCheck.call().
getState())
  }
```

I'm able to inject the health check into other parts of the application and use as I see fit. Neat!

Fault Tolerance

Can your microservice platform take a punch? Can it survive blips in network connectivity? Will it fall apart during a momentary pause in response from a dependency? How will it fail when it's overwhelmed by demand? These are just some of the rude surprises in store for application designers that are new to highly distributed and cloud environments, especially when you're coming from an on-premise deployment of monoliths, where you're used to being in control of every piece of the monolith. You can coordinate and deploy everything you need as a single block. If you're moving to the microservice architecture, your application must be able to not implode after an HTTP request times out. No, several layers of `try-with-resources` don't count.

Figure 3-6. *Pictured: your microservices after a database insert gone wrong*

To build adult-tier microservices, try on the MicroProfile Fault Tolerance API, by way of the `quarkus-smallrye-fault-tolerance` extension. MicroProfile's fault tolerance strategy revolves around five annotations:

- `@Timeout` to manage the wait time before reporting failure.

- `@Retry` to define retry tactics for failed executions.

- `@Fallback` to define alternative handling steps in the event of a failure.

117

- @Bulkhead to control the limits of concurrent access to a method; helps to prevent overwhelming the resource. This can help implement the Staged Event Driven Architecture, one of my favorite design patterns. It's a solid way to manage the throughput to asynchronous methods.

- @CircuitBreaker to fail fast where applicable.

These annotations can all be inherited, so you can use these as a way to enforce default behavior for failure conditions in a codebase. Here's some of that in action:

```
@GET
@Path("/hello-image")
@Operation(summary = "Returns an image")
@Produces("image/jpg")
@Retry(delay = 2000,delayUnit = ChronoUnit.MILLIS,maxRetries =
4, retryOn = {SocketTimeoutException.class, ConnectException.
class}) (1)
@Asynchronous (2a)
@Bulkhead(value = 10,waitingTaskQueue = 30) (2b)
@Timeout(value=5000,unit=ChronoUnit.MILLIS) (3)
public CompletionStage<byte[]> helloImage() throws
InterruptedException, ExecutionException {
    CompletionStage<byte[]> futureImage = httpBinService.
    getImageAsync();
    byte[] imageBytes = futureImage.toCompletableFuture().get();
    return Response.ok().entity(new StreamingOutput() {
        @Override
        public void write(OutputStream output)
            throws IOException, WebApplicationException {
                output.write(imageBytes);
```

```
            output.flush();
        }
    }).build();
    }
    return futureImage
}
```

1. @Retry on this resource method stipulates that this method should be retried four times, with a delay of 2 seconds between each attempt. The retries should be attempted only in the event of a SocketTimeoutException or a ConnectionException.

2. There are two parts to @Bulkhead usage. It can be defined on its own or with

   a. @org.eclipse.microprofile.faulttolerance. Asynchronous to pool excess requests.

   b. This will now allow ten concurrent requests and a backlog of 30 waiting for processing. Any more and a BulkHeadException will be thrown.

   I use @Timeout to stipulate that this method should wait five seconds before the execution is marked a failure.

The MicroProfile specification integrates this standard with the REST client specification as well, so that I can have

```
@RegisterProvider(LoggingFilter.class)
@RegisterProvider(HttpBinExceptionMapper.class)
@RegisterRestClient(baseUri = "https://httpbin.org/")
@RegisterForReflection
public interface HttpBinServiceDAO{
```

```
@GET
@Path("/image/jpeg")
@Produces("image/jpeg")
@Timeout(value = 5000,unit = ChronoUnit.MILLIS)
CompletionStage<byte[]> getImageAsync();
}
```

@Timeout configures a 5000ms timeout for this REST client call, after which a TimeoutException will be thrown. Be ready with an ExceptionHandler and ExceptionMapper.

Reactive Programming with Vert.x

Eclipse's Vert.x is a toolkit for building high-performing, scalable, reactive applications. What's reactive programming? Think of reactive programming as a model of programming that combines

- Asynchronous programming

- A fluent API

- Event-driven programming

- CPU/core-efficient threading

If you've been through some of the chapters before this one, you may have seen CompletionStage already – that's a reactive class provided by the JDK. One difference between CompletionStage and say java.util. concurrent.Future is that with Future, you're responsible for checking that the operation is complete; CompletionStage will *react* to the presence of the expected output data or execute any exception handling callbacks you implement.

Vert.x operates in the same space as CompletionStage. Quarkus uses *a lot* of Vert.x under the covers; you'll see [vert.x-worker-thread] in your console, for example. A core principle in Vert.x is *non-blocking*, for that sweet, sweet performance boost. When you're using anything Vert.x related – within or outside of Quarkus – you should opt for a reactive or asynchronous programming model. Vert.x can do everything I've demonstrated so far in this book: rest clients, reactive rest service endpoints, and so on. Let me show you some things that I haven't tried yet.

High-Performance Netty with Vert.x

Like with most application servers, you have the option of using native connectors. The connector is the component that helps your Tomcat, Jetty, or Netty server accept and process incoming connections. Going with a *native* connector is basically supercharging the process of connection thread handling. Native connectors typically use the Java Native Interface (JNI) to skip the middleman and deal directly with the operating system.

You can get Netty on steroids by adding the following maven dependencies to your project:

```
<dependency>
  <groupId>io.netty</groupId>
  <artifactId>netty-transport-native-epoll</artifactId>
  <classifier>linux-x86_64</classifier>
</dependency>
<dependency>
  <groupId>io.netty</groupId>
  <artifactId>netty-transport-native-kqueue</artifactId>
  <classifier>osx-x86_64</classifier>
</dependency>
```

There's currently only support for either Mac OS X or Linux operating systems for these. Netty will select the appropriate connector based on the deployment environment. You then enable native transport with `quarkus.`

`vertx.prefer-native-transport=true` in your *application.properties*. Also in your *application.properties*, you can tune the following parameters:

- `quarkus.http.so-reuse-port=true` controls how the OS will provision listener threads for inbound sockets on your web server. Enabling this allows Linux sockets to independently monitor for incoming data, a possible throughput boost.

- `quarkus.http.tcp-quick-ack` controls the behavior of packet sending by the OS. Typically, network I/O in your machine will have either delayed acknowledgment (DELAYED_ACK) or Nagle's algorithm to prevent immediate transmission of small packets. Disabling delayed acknowledgment with "quick ack" forces the machine to send packets immediately available. This could be useful for low-latency requirements.

- `quarkus.http.tcp-cork=true` controls the behavior of the network layer in conjunction with delaying algorithms like Nagle's algorithm. Nagle's is a TCP/IP algorithm that delays transmission of data until a buffer has filled to a configurable limit – it's the opposite of "quick ack". This makes it more efficient with bandwidth as you're not clogging the network with too many small chunks of data. TCP corking will then aggressively accumulate data into the buffer, waiting for a max of 200ms before flushing.

- `quarkus.http.tcp-fast-open` will enable TCP Fast Open, a TCP feature that allows Netty skip some formalities in the TCP handshake algorithm; this improves latency.

Tip   Quarkus provides the `quarkus.thread-pool.core-threads` property (default = 1) to tune the number of threads in the worker pool. Tune this and the other `quarkus.thread-pool.*` properties to bang out even better throughput and latency from your quarkus app.

Reactive Messaging with Vert.x

An event bus is like an information superhighway. It's a trunk of information that runs through an entire application. Interested parties just need to plug in to the bus and

- Publish messages to multiple receivers (publish-subscribe)

- Send messages in a fire-and-forget fashion

- Send messages targeted at specific components or destination

- Send messages and expect a response (request-reply)

- Receive messages at their desired addresses

The challenge usually is that traditional buses are resource-thirsty, heavyweight components that require a bunch of infrastructural change. The likes of CDI and Spring attempt something like this, but they're type-dependent and can't be targeted that well. Not to mention the absence of reactivity. No more! Vert.x provides an embeddable event bus that embodies all the design goals of reactive programming. I'll first add the Vert.x extension to my project with `quarkus-vertx`.

Vert.x programming in Quarkus is underpinned by SmallRye Mutiny. Mutiny is a streamlined and simplified reactive programming API. The folks behind Mutiny took one look at the bajillion methods in RxJava and the like, and said "*Nyet*". Mutiny is a much more digestible and practical approach to reactive programming in Java, supporting most common use cases with none of the fat. I'll add the Mutiny extension to my project with `quarkus-resteasy-mutiny`.

At the core of Mutiny are the `Uni` and `Multi` classes, which provide the entrypoints into its reactive API. I can return an instance of either one, instead of returning a `CompletionStage`. So, my earlier reactive example could be rewritten as

```
@GET
@Path("/{name:[a-zA-Z]*}/scramble-mutiny")
public Uni<Response> getMutinyAnagram(final @PathParam("name")
String name) {
        return Uni.createFrom().item(name).onItem().
        apply(toScramble -> {
            return Response.ok(getAnagram(toScramble)).
            type(MediaType.APPLICATION_JSON).build(); });
}
```

The general approach is to take a given data item – a `String` or a `Collection`, whatever – and create a `Uni` or `Multi` from it. From there, supply your desired business logic into the apply method. This is a more comfortable reactive API – it has a very small fraction of the methods that the bloated, popular APIs do – without sacrificing functionality. `Uni` provides handling for single items. Use `Multi` for a collection of items. My returning a `Uni` from getMutinyAnagram causes Quarkus to engage reactive mode.

Mutiny is compatible with the popular reactive frameworks, like RxJava, Standard JDK `CompletionStage`, and so on. For many other components in Quarkus, you can return either of the two types and

Quarkus will implicitly engage reactive mode. SQL and NoSQL database access, security functions, and message brokers all have reactive options by way of Mutiny. Enjoy!

Vert.x Event Bus

And now, for my next trick, I'm going to show you how to send messages reactively, across your application! First, I'll get a hold of the event bus:

```
io.vertx.mutiny.core.eventbus.EventBus :
@Inject
EventBus eventBus;
```

I can now use this bus to send messages all over the Quarkus app, **across a cluster** (if your app is deployed in a cluster) or just locally, all in a very lightweight and CPU-efficient manner:

```
@POST
@Path("/send-event")
@Consumes("application/json")
public void sendEvent(EventMessage message) throws
InterruptedException, ExecutionException{
    eventBus.publish("multi-cast", message); (1)
    DeliveryOptions options = new DeliveryOptions(); (2)
    options.addHeader("send-time", Instant.now().
    toString())
            .setLocalOnly(true)
            .setSendTimeout(2000);

    eventBus.request("one-way-message", message, options); (3)
    eventBus.request("", message).on().item().
    apply(responseMessage -> {
```

```
        logger.info("Blocking two-way response received.
        Address " + responseMessage.address() + ", message:
        " + responseMessage.body()
        );
        return responseMessage.body();
    }); (4)

    Message<Object> response = eventBus.request(
    "two-way-message", message.getMessage()).subscribe()
    .asCompletionStage().get(); (5)
    logger.info("Non-blocking two-way response: " +
    response.body());
    }
}
```

Alright, here goes:

1. This is a basic message publish, sending the
   message to all listeners subscribed to the
   "multi-cast" address.

2. Because Vertx's event bus isn't a pretender of a
   messaging bus, you get the trappings of a proper
   message-driven architecture. Here I'm preparing
   metadata to send along with the actual message
   payload.

3. I can send a one-way, fire-and-forget message to
   an arbitrary endpoint called "one-way-message",
   enriched with metadata.

4. All of this can be reactive as well – I can send to a
   targeted endpoint in a reactive fashion.

5. Now I can send a message targeted at a single endpoint with a request-reply model. Note how I convert back to a CompletionStage, still a reactive component.

This is all well and good for the sending of messages. How about the receiving end?

```
...
import io.vertx.mutiny.core.Vertx;
import io.vertx.mutiny.core.eventbus.Message;
import io.quarkus.vertx.ConsumeEvent;

    import org.acme.dto.EventMessage

...
@ApplicationScoped (1)
public class EventBusMessageRecipient{

    @Inject
    Vertx vertx;(2)

    final Logger logger = LoggerFactory.getLogger(EventBus
    MessageRecipient.class.getName());

    @ConsumeEvent("one-way-message")(3)
    public void receiveOneWayMessage(Message<EventMessage>
    message){
        logger.info("Received one way message: "+message.
        body().getMessage());
    }
```

```
@ConsumeEvent("two-way-message")
public EventMessage receiveTwoWayMessage(String message){
    logger.info("Received two-way message "+message);
    EventMessage response = new EventMessage(); //this is a
    custom type, not a special Vert.x component
    response.setMessage("Message received");
    return response;
}

@ConsumeEvent("multi-cast")
public void coReceiveOneWayMessage(Message<EventMessage>
message){
    logger.info("Received broadcast message");
}

@ConsumeEvent("multi-cast")
public void coReceiveOneWayMessage(EventMessage message){
    logger.info("Received broadcast message "+message.
    getMessage());
}

@ConsumeEvent("blocking-two-way-message",blocking=true)
public void receiveBlockingTwoWayMessage(Message<String>
message){
    logger.info("Message received in blocking handler:
    "+message.body());
    vertx.setTimer(5, timeout ->{ (4)
        logger.info("Sending response after "+timeout);
        message.reply("Here's the response");
    });
}
}
```

1. The `@ApplicationScoped` means there will be just one instance of this bean in this context, effectively a singleton.

2. The `Vertx` object is the entirety of Vert.x as made available in Quarkus. It's an immensely powerful component. I can't overstate how much you can do with this component – the thing has an in-memory File System. Check out the `Vert.x documentation` for a glimpse of how powerful Vert.x is.

3. The `@ConsumeEvent` annotation defines the address that this method will pick up messages from. You have the option of

   a. Not responding when a message is sent

   b. Responding by returning a return value from the method

   c. Responding by setting the response on the `Message` wrapper class

4. I'm using the Vert.x engine here to simulate a delay of 5 seconds, before sending back a response. Yes, I know I could also do `Thread.sleep()`, but this is so much cooler!

This is an extremely rudimentary example of what you can do with the `EventBus` and Vert.x as a whole. Vert.x is programming-language agnostic,[10] can be clustered, and uses SSL all within a microservice. Power!

---

[10]The official documentation recommends JSON as the preferred message format so that anything downstream can read the message. I'm opting for a custom data type here to show that you can send anything you want.

Microservice Success with Quarkus

Listen, this is a book on microservices quite alright, but you should understand that going the microservice route is not a panacea. While it solves specific challenges attributable directly to monoliths, it introduces a new set of challenges directly attributable to the fine-grained nature of microservices. Breaking a monolith into microservices is a sort of balkanization of your platform: where you had just a handful of moving parts, you'll now have ten, hundreds, or even more, all vying for resources and attention; they will all come up with a rich and diverse array of ways to fail.

Figure 3-7. *Pictured: your unsupervised microservices working together*

You'll need to reconsider your approach to

- **Scalability and resiliency**: A true microservice architecture is more granular. You're going to be managing more endpoints and more black box dependencies. Fault tolerance is a must if you're going the microservice route. Expect everything your microservice depends on to fail. Consider using highly available and resilient messaging with Apache Kafka or something similar to help buffer inter-service communication. It's also no coincidence that everything in Quarkus is reactive – that really is the best option for scalability. Go reactive wherever you can afford it.

- **Configuration management**: With that many moving parts, properly maintaining the properties and configuration that your service depends on will need to be a priority. One of the proposals of microservice architecture is that you should be able to swap out a microservice for a new version, without breaking flow. Robust and secure configuration management needs to be part of the conversation early on. Quarkus provides extension support for HashiCorp's Vault, a secure storage and transport mechanism to help manage artifacts like SSL certificates, credentials, and other sensitive configuration items that your microservice needs to function.

- **Production support**: You'll need to up your game with regard to your operational support capabilities. Effective logging, Mapped Diagnostic Context (MDC) logging, and distributed traceability should be top of the list if you're going micro. That goes double for machine-friendly logging with JSON. With so many moving parts, it's going to be more difficult to diagnose production issues. Quarkus provides support for all that and more. Consider the Quarkus support for OpenTracing to enable distributed tracing in your application. The Quarkus metrics extension provides support for OpenMetrics as well, to give you a real-time feed of the health of your applications. This data can then be fed to application performance monitoring platforms like Prometheus or Datadog.

TL;DR: Site reliability engineering (SRE) needs to be front and center in your microservice transition.

Don't think you *must* go all in on microservices either. There's a middle ground between the monolith and granular microservices. Quarkus has you covered for the entire spectrum!

CHAPTER 4

Packaging and Deploying Quarkus Applications

Typically, technical textbooks save the "packaging and deployment" talk for last, like vegetables on a dinner plate full of meat. I'm bringing it up front, because when we're talking Quarkus, the deployment options are like half the point. This will be worth your while.

The cloud presents a new frontier and new challenges for packaging and deploying microservices. Microservices are so hot right now, but way too many aren't prepared for the change. Now, the haters have said many hurtful things about Java: how big java deployment kits are, how much RAM a Java application needs, and how slow it is. Really unkind stuff. In the cloud-everything world, these criticisms of Java become real hazards. Take Amazon Web Services (AWS), for example: a lot of the pricing models of their services revolve around two things.

- CPU: How much CPU time your code or application requires

- RAM: How much RAM your code consumes; its memory footprint

© Tayo Koleoso 2020

T. Koleoso, *Beginning Quarkus Framework*, https://doi.org/10.1007/978-1-4842-6032-6_4

From the AWS Lambda service pricing page itself:

*With AWS Lambda, you pay only for what you use. **You are** **charged based on** the number of requests for your functions and the duration, **the time it takes for your code to execute** ... Duration is calculated from the time your code begins executing until it returns or otherwise terminates, rounded up to the nearest 100ms*...**An increase in memory size triggers an equivalent increase in CPU available to your function**.*

Translation: You're going to spend, spend, spend, if your application takes a "long" time to start or needs a bunch of RAM. Even CPU-efficient code that requires more RAM will wind up costing more because more RAM triggers more CPU allocation from AWS. Having code that starts sharply and consumes relatively little RAM can be the difference between running a service for free in AWS and skipping meals so you can afford to fund your startup. At the scale of a large enterprise, the multiplier effect is even more obvious. An organization that's serving millions of requests a day in cloud infrastructure will start to see the hit to their bottom line when they're spending a bunch of money in cloud operation costs. The way cloud pricing models are written on paper, you'd think "it's just $0.0000008333 per GB/second. Doesn't sound like much". Multiply that enough times at scale, and you'll start seeing your departmental heads asking questions about cost.

Let's even leave the money out of it for now; suggesting that one can run a Java application in an embedded deployment environment has always raised eyebrows. "Are you sure Java is not too heavy to use in a Raspberry Pi?"; "Java is too slow to use in low-latency systems". Individuals and organizations have had to make language and platform switches from Java to others, after considering the historical resource requirements of the Java platform.

So here we are with a supersonic subatomic platform promising to show them all. And show them, we shall. For my next demonstration, I'm going to kit up my Quarkus project with the following features:

- PostgreSQL driver

- Hibernate, with all the trimmings

- Agroal connection pool manager

- MicroProfile health

- MicroProfile metrics

- MicroProfile REST client

- REST support

- Narayana transaction manager

- JSON marshaling support

- Reactive transport

- JWT

- Scheduled batch processing

Between all these, you have the ingredients for a production-strength application. Let me show you the differences in outcome.

JVM Mode

There's nothing fancy going on here. Deploying your Quarkus app in JVM mode simply refers to the vanilla Java way of running a JAR-red up application. You build the JAR:

```
mvn clean install
```

and you run it:

```
java -jar <app name.jar>. quarkus.package.output-name
```

That's it. Oh wait, one more thing: configure the quarkus.package.output-name property in the application.properties file to control the name of the output file from the build.

Native Mode

You know what a JAR is.[1] Most, if not all, Java applications are fundamentally composed of JARs. Sure, you'll have your WAR, but really, it's still just an aggregation of JARs with some configuration files thrown in. JARs containing Java classes are the way they are, because they were conceived in a WORA world where the JVM is expected to lug a bunch of fat around. You get to download/add a JAR to your project and just use it – no need to worry about any OS-specific conditions that could cause your code to work differently. At least that's what the intention was. As you now know, that flexibility comes at the cost of speed and resource efficiency.

Native code is what you get when you don't have to worry about any of that cross-OS overcompensation. You know all the classes and JVM resources your application will need. You also know what your target deployment environment is – serverless, containerized, embedded, whatever – you should be able to target your code for that platform. On a Windows machine, that's a .exe in Window, and a .dimg in macOS. This is what native code is all about. And it isn't just sales-speak; Observe: this is a traditional java-built Quarkus application's startup:

```
04:49:21 INFO  [io.quarkus] (main) code-with-quarkus
1.0.0-SNAPSHOT (powered by Quarkus 1.5.0.Final) started in
2.285s. Listening on: http://0.0.0.0:8081
```

---

[1]Don't you?

```
04:49:21 INFO  [io.quarkus] (main) Profile prod activated.
04:49:21 INFO  [io.quarkus] (main) Installed features: [agroal,
cdi, hibernate-orm, hibernate-orm-panache, jdbc-postgresql,
mutiny, narayana-jta, rest-client, resteasy, resteasy-jsonb,
scheduler, security, servlet, smallrye-context-propagation,
smallrye-health, smallrye-jwt, smallrye-metrics, smallrye-
openapi, vertx, vertx-web]
```

started in 2.285 seconds. That's after a bunch of warm-up startups, by the way. In the serverless or low-latency worlds, that might as well be an hour. Here's *exactly* the same Quarkus code, with the same Quarkus dependencies, but now compiled as a native image:

```
04:34:46 INFO  [io.quarkus] (main) code-with-quarkus
1.0.0-SNAPSHOT (powered by Quarkus 1.5.0.Final) started in
0.028s. Listening on: http://0.0.0.0:8083
04:34:46 INFO  [io.quarkus] (main) Profile prod activated.
04:34:46 INFO  [io.quarkus] (main) Installed features: [agroal,
cdi, hibernate-orm, hibernate-orm-panache, jdbc-postgresql,
mutiny, narayana-jta, rest-client, resteasy, resteasy-jsonb,
scheduler, security, servlet, smallrye-context-propagation,
smallrye-health, smallrye-jwt, smallrye-metrics, smallrye-
openapi, vertx, vertx-web]
```

started in 0.028 seconds! The Quarkus native image started up **81** times faster than the traditional JVM version; my jaw dropped the first time I saw this. The likes of Spring Boot couldn't possibly compete with this, without going native themselves. How about RAM and CPU consumption?

App Mode	CPU%	RAM (MB)	% of Total RAM
JVM mode	0.3	381.13	10.1
Native mode	0.0	53.97	1.4

Look at that. It bears repeating: this is the same Quarkus project, with the same dependencies running in two different modes; both instances are at rest, not serving any requests. These are Nürburgring-worthy numbers, from the platform some would call "slow". I feel like the lead character in that movie, Moneyball (I think Brad Moneyball was his name[2]). It's not even close: while the traditional Java app is eating up **10.1%** of available memory,[3] the native image is using **1.4%, a more than 700% difference in memory consumption.** Where the traditional Quarkus app is using **0.3%** of CPU, the native image is not even registering at all. It gets even more impressive when you realize that, thanks to Quarkus optimizations for the target JVM, JVM mode Quarkus apps are already better performing than some of the competition.

What did I do to get the code to this point? Not too much. Let's meet the main player in all of this.

GraalVM

GraalVM is a high-performance, polyglot JVM distributed by Oracle. You can get it at `www.graalvm.org/downloads`. It aims to be the JVM for all seasons and languages.

The secret sauce in GraalVM is an ability to take your `.java` file, straight to operating system-specific machine code, the so-called native image. For Windows, you'll get a .exe; for *nix, you'll get a Unix executable. It is partially this wizardry that makes GraalVM unique among JVMs. GraalVM works with a set of tools and utilities to generate an OS-specific image that will do all that magic that I showed in the previous section. With those OS-specific tools, GraalVM scans your project's code and maps out every class, method, and JVM feature that's referenced in your code, directly or indirectly. It's then able to AOT-compile the entire dependency tree and

---

[2]Editor's note: You haven't watched that movie, have you?
[3]This was captured from Unix's top utility.

produce the native image that contains strictly what your code needs and nothing else. With Quarkus, it can also include resource and configuration files in that image. What you get at the end of it is a single deployment unit that you can run on the target OS.

GraalVM started off as a component in the Hotspot VM – the VM you're probably most familiar with. Oracle then excised it from the standard VM and made it its own stand-alone VM – so you now have the privilege of paying for an "Enterprise" version. Don't get me wrong, the Community Edition of GraalVM is fine as a standard VM as well – you can run any Java applications in it as normal without any of the native business and still get superior performance to the standard Hotspot. The latest incarnation of GraalVM now ships a Maven plugin that lets you cut out the middleman a little bit. The Maven plugin allows you to compile your code and generate a native image using the native image tool, all in one step.

Additionally, Red Hat has announced the Mandrel project, a Red Hat sponsored and supported build of GraalVM. With Mandrel, Red Hat offers features and support for Graal that you might not get from the Oracle-supplied GraalVM.

Now back to Quarkus! Ideally, you should only need to download and configure GraalVM and run the following Maven command on your Quarkus project:

```
mvn package -Pnative
```

The reality is that reliably generating native images with Quarkus is not as straightforward as I would like. Also, I don't recommend doing it in the standard "development environment" way and here's why:

- GraalVM as distributed directly by Oracle doesn't "just work" because you downloaded it. To get the native image generation capability, there's some configuration to do – not to mention having to manually install some of the tools it needs, which to me is a hassle.

139

- As at the time of this writing, support for Windows is
  experimental (read: it's probably not going to work
  for you in many cases); Windows devs aren't going to
  have a good time. I should know: one of my personal
  development computers' Windows machine.[4]

- **WORP:** You should be compiling the native image in
  the operating system for which you're targeting the
  image. What's going to be the point of building a native
  image in Windows, for example, for an application
  destined for a Unix environment? No es bueno.
  Predictability is key.

So, to recap, trying to get Quarkus apps natively generated on my raw
Windows development environment was not fun. The first problem I ran
into was some video drivers conflicting with the native image generator
utility in Graal. Being the lazy developer that I am, I'm interested in this
only if it's plug-n-play – everything should come bundled and ready to run.

Tip   Java Reflection and Native mode are at odds: Native mode
operates on so-called "closed-world" basis; it requires being able
to compile all the classes and dependencies that a Java app needs
ahead of time. Wanton reflection is the opposite of that – it's *all
about* dynamic class loading. Quarkus closes this gap by providing
the @RegisterForReflection annotation. Add this annotation
to classes that will be candidates for reflection, for example, DTO
classes that will be used for requests and responses in REST
endpoints.

---

[4]Don't judge me!

Native Java Image Limitations

Because we can't have nice things. We know by now that native imagery requires upfront knowledge about what your Java application is going to need. Some other things you should know about generating native images with GraalVM are

- Native images don't do automatic heap or thread dump capture, which sucks for the site reliability engineering (SRE) folk.

- Analyzing and AOT-compiling every class and dependency your application needs takes time and RAM. At a minimum, you're going to need over 1G free RAM to complete a native compilation of a relatively small application. Configure `quarkus.native.native-image-xmx` in your application.properties to increase the RAM allocation for the native image.

- Monitoring and management via JMX is limited. *Fortunately*, MicroProfile provides the Metrics API, so you're not flying blind. You will be able to expose your microservices to Prometheus and any other platform that implements the OpenMetrics standard. You can also use VisualVM to monitor your native application; you just won't be able to trigger a heap dump from it. Add `-H:+AllowVMInspection` or `quarkus.native.enable-vm-inspection=true` to expose your application to introspection.

- At the time of this writing, there's limited support for the Java Flight Recorder (JFR) in GraalVM. JFR is my favorite JDK tool, by the way. The GraalVM team is working on improving support for JFR incrementally, so I don't expect this to be a long-lasting limitation.

141

- Native images aren't suited for applications that will trigger frequent garbage collection. Native imagery uses a serial garbage collector which isn't the most efficient garbage collector. You can mitigate this by sizing and partitioning your heap sufficiently, to minimize the need for frequent garbage collection.

- There could be a slight increase in latency when running a Quarkus Java application in native mode. Nothing too bad; the serial garbage collector is not helping. You should performance test your native image application.

- To get past these limitations, you'll need to pay Oracle[5] for the enterprise version of GraalVM.

Overall, 9/10 recommend, #teamquarkus all the way. I pay a one-time upfront cost for continuous resource savings in production? Sign me up! The performance boost and cost savings make it all worth it.

Native Imagery in DevOps

Whether you're running CircleCI, Jenkins, or something else, in most enterprises, build servers are shared infrastructure. The disk space, RAM, and CPU resources being used to build deployment kits need to be managed across many users and build jobs.

Quarkus' native compilation is a hungry hungry hippo as I've already established. In a continuous integration/continuous deployment (CI/CD) shop, y'all have got to be mindful of how your builds affect others. Already it's expected that an organization that takes CI/CD seriously must be

---

[5]*And may Larry Ellison be with you.*

prepared to allocate significant resources to a build server. This need will increase significantly if you're introducing native mode compilation. To that end

- Size your worker thread pools with the expectation that a single native build job could hold onto one thread for north of an hour. I've seen it happen. As a project grows to use more extensions or even more code, the length of time it'll take to native compile is likely to grow. There's a risk that native build jobs will starve their neighbors of CPU time.

- The rate of growth of RAM requirements of a job is not linear; it could be exponential. The more extensions introduced to the project, the greater the thirst for build-time RAM. Some extensions will require less than others. Introducing some dependencies could double the RAM requirement overnight. If you've followed every example in this book up till this point, your Quarkus project will require a minimum of 2.5GB of free RAM to native compile.

- If you run a pipeline where you run unit or integration tests as part of the build process, consider using the JVM mode deployment for the tests and only run the native image tests at the tail end of the release train. Alternatively, configure the `quarkus.test.native-image-wait-time` property to set a time limit for image building during a test run.

- Configure `quarkus.native.native-image-xmx` to limit the maximum amount of memory native image generation can consume.

- Consider *containerized* build jobs. This way, each build in Jenkins is isolated and predictable. You can also manage the RAM utilization per build job with more granularity and oversight.

An ideal build setup will be able to bundle everything that you'll ever need for building native images in one neat package. The package should contain

- GraalVM, installed and configured

- Maven, installed and configured

- The native image tool, installed and configured

How does one get essentially a running operating system, with software installed and preconfigured? Because really, all I want to do is drop my code somewhere and have my code converted into a native image, predictably and reliably. All of this stuff should...just work!

Enter containerization!

A Crash Course in Containerization

If you're new to containerization and you're a java developer, here's the elevator pitch using Docker as the basis.

Docker is like a JVM for whole operating systems. A near-complete operating system environment is packaged as an "image" (like APIs and Java applications are packaged as JARs) and you can download the images to your local machine. An image you download to your local machine is a near-complete operating system (OS) bundle, and there are thousands of them. Just like you don't need to worry about the implementation details of a JAR most of the time, you are generally able to pull down docker images and use them as is.

This concept is what the nerds call "containerization": download a Docker image of an OS configured with anything you desire; run an instance of that image – called a "container" – inside the docker runtime; use it like you have another OS running inside your OS (your OS/machine is called the "host" in Docker-speak).

"But isn't that just virtualization with extra steps?", you ask in an oddly high-pitched voice, for some reason. Containerization with Docker serves a similar purpose as virtualization, but it offers far more portability and flexibility than vanilla virtualization. Think of the difference between containerization and virtualization this way: containerization is like using a JAR – on its own, a JAR is a completely functional, independent unit and ready to use. Virtualization is more akin to handing a third party your source code and the entire IDE you developed the code in. It's not as portable is what I'm saying.

Hint   Just like JARs in Java, it can be used to either package complete, functional applications that are ready to use or they can be used to package APIs that you can build your own applications on; Docker images are either complete and ready to use as is or you can build your own images on top of other images.

How does any of this help with generating native Quarkus images? Remember how much of a hassle it could be to set up a native image capable GraalVM installation? And how counter-WORP it is to generate native code on your local development OS? What I need now is a docker image that comes preconfigured with GraalVM and all the tools it needs to do its thing. With that, I should only need to

- Download the image and run it as a container

- Copy my code into the running container

- Use it to generate a native image of my Quarkus application

Remember Container images are functional OSes, so when I generate a native image, that image is targeted to the OS that the container is running. First thing to do is to install Docker on your machine. Docker is the "JVM" in this scenario; first we get the "JVM," then we get the "JAR" or images to use in it.

Don't worry if you've never done this before – this is why you bought this book.

Install Docker

www.docker.com is where you go for your Docker installation. To keep things simple, just download Docker Desktop and follow the instructions to install.

Configure Docker

After successfully installing Docker, two things need configuring:

- **File System sharing**: For me, to be able to transmit my code, written inside my IDE, into a docker container, I need to expose my local File System to the Docker runtime. Go to **Settings ➤ Resources ➤ File System** to configure the paths or path that you'd like to expose to the Docker runtime.

- **Machine resource configuration:** This one bit me. The process of generating a native image is CPU and RAM intensive and takes a lot longer than I'm used to with traditional Java code compilation. For this reason, it's important to allocate enough RAM and CPU to the Docker runtime. Without doing this, you may find that the native image generation step seems to stall and error out mysteriously. If you're on a resource-poor machine, you can hold off on this until you hit that wall, if you do at all. Otherwise, it's something to be aware of. Go to **Settings ➤ Resources ➤ Advanced** and tweak the numbers there based on your needs.

Having installed Docker, I can validate my installation by opening a terminal or command-line window and running the following command:

```
docker info
```

This command prints diagnostic information about the installation and the OS environment. Now that I have my OS "JVM," I need "JARs" or docker images to run in it. You can also run `docker run hello-world` to download and run a "hello-world" image, as proof that all is well.

Install the CentOS Image

Docker images are collected in image repositories or registries, much like Java JARs are collected in Artifactory, Nexus, or the global Maven repo. Traditionally, you would go to `hub.docker.com` to search for any images you want. Images are created and published with relevant info to that site. Vendors like Oracle, Redis, and even individuals like you and I can publish images containing canned OSes with preconfigured distributions of their products. Users can then go and "pull" those images into their deployment machines and run the images as containers. What I want now is a complete Linux distribution that comes with GraalVM, all its dependencies and tooling preconfigured, native imager installed, and Maven.

Meet `https://quay.io`. The Quarkus team has distributed several useful images to the `docker images` at the command line to see the list of images available in the docker runtime. Here's what it looks like for me:

```
REPOSITORY                                      TAG
IMAGE ID           CREATED                      SIZE
quay.io/quarkus/centos-quarkus-maven            20.0.0-java11
39d6594a5a6a           15 hours ago             1.86GB
quay.io/quarkus/ubi-quarkus-native-image        20.0.0-java11
91fb19e82ebc           16 hours ago             1.43GB
```

Now that we have an image, let's start a container based on that image.

Run the CentOS Image

Let's fire up a container from the CentOS image. When I "run" an image, I'm telling the Docker runtime that I want a virtual operating system running on my machine, using the image as the template. So, from my CentOS image, I want CentOS and all the goodies bundled within to start up on my PC. To make this a fulfilling run, I'd like a couple more things:

- I want my Quarkus project code to be made available inside the virtual OS. I want changes I make in my local File System reflected inside the containerized OS.

- Since the container I want to run is a fully self-contained computer, running inside my own computer, I should be able to run my Quarkus code *inside* the container. Not just that, but from my own environment outside the docker container, I should be able to send REST requests to the Quarkus service running inside the container.

Here's the command that does all that:

```
docker run -it --name my-quarkus-app -p 8080:8080 -v
//c/eclipse-workspace/code-with-quarkus:/my-quarkus/app quay.
io/quarkus/centos-quarkus-maven:20.0.0-java11  bash -l
```

Here's the breakdown of "all that":

1. docker is the actual docker tool – can't do anything without this.

2. run command to run the image.

3. -it asks the tool for an interactive session.

4. -p stipulates that when a request hits 8080 on my host machine, it should be forwarded to port 8080 inside the docker container. This way, I can initiate REST resource requests from my dev environment and have them executed by the code running inside the fake computer I'm about to start.

5. -v tells the docker runtime to take C:\eclipse-workspace\code-with-quarkus and mirror it as /my-quarkus/app, inside the virtual computer I'm about to run. This option makes my project code available inside the container. This way, changes I make in C:\eclipse-workspace\code-with-quarkus will be reflected inside /my-quarkus/app directory in the container and vice versa.

6. quay.io/quarkus/centos-quarkus-maven is the fully qualified name of the CentOS docker image, kinda like saying javax.ws.rs.core.Application, instead of just Application. 20.0.0-java11 is the version of this image that I want to use. Be sure to check quay.io for the latest version of this image, in case version 20.0.0-java11 has been deprecated by the time you get this book.

7. bash instructs the Docker engine to immediately launch a bash shell session inside the container as soon as it has been created.

You should be able to substitute your own values into the various command positions and run the command as is.

Inside the newly created container's bash shell, I should be able to check to be sure certain things are available and configured in this OS. From inside the open bash shell:

1. Check that maven is installed with `mvn -v`:

   ```
   OpenJDK 64-Bit Server VM warning: forcing
   TieredStopAtLevel to full optimization because
   JVMCI is enabled
   Apache Maven 3.6.3
   (cecedd343002696d0abb50b32b541b8a6ba2883f)
   Maven home: /usr/share/maven
   ...
   ```

2. Check that GraalVM is installed with echo $JAVA_HOME:

   ```
   [quarkus@1eaf2b1b569f project]$ echo $JAVA_HOME
   /opt/graalvm
   ```

3. Confirm that my code is available inside the OS by navigating to the directory I mounted.

If everything is looking good, on to the next step.

Build Native Images Inside a Docker Container

From this point on, it's straightforward. First navigate to your project directory inside the bash shell

```
cd /my-quarkus/app
```

then run the following command to generate the native image:

```
mvn package -Pnative -DskipTests
```

This is what begins the compilation and generation process. If you're the curious type, add `-X` and `-e` flags to the maven command to see debug-level information while the image generation executes. If it fails for non-compilation or dependency-related reasons, the most likely suspect is host OS resources. This is why I recommended that you allocate enough RAM to the Docker Desktop app. The native image generation is RAM intensive – it's a lot of upfront hard work. Allocate more RAM and run it again. *When* all goes well, you should have a native image generated in the /target subdirectory (it's the file without an extension). It's the file without an extension: code-with-quarkus-1.0.0-SNAPSHOT-runner.[6]

Hint   Compare the sizes of the artifacts generated from native images and what you get from JVM mode JARs. The native image is slightly bigger than the complete JVM jar.

Native image secured. Fire it up:

```
./code-with-quarkus-1.0.0-SNAPSHOT-runner
```

I should now be able to hit the RESTful service deployed inside the container, from within my host operating system. It's this native image that becomes your deployment package, targeted Unix/Linux environments. I've personally validated the generated image, not only in CentOS but also in Red Hat and Ubuntu Linux distros. Not only is this good to run in related distros of Linux; it no longer needs the JDK or JRE to run – not even GraalVM needs to be present once the native image has been generated. It's now a self-contained executable with amazing throughput. All of this to lead to the holy grail: a small, lightweight java application that can run in resource-starved environments. Quarkus gives you flexibility and control of the native image generation process with a bunch of configuration options.

---

[6]**Remember**: the quarkus.package.output-name property controls the name of the output file.

Build Native Images with Maven: A Shortcut

Muahahahahah! Yes, there's a one-step way to generate native images, using Docker, but without having to manually go inside the container and execute mvn package -Pnative. Are you ready? Okay, here goes:

```
mvn package -Pnative -Dquarkus.native.container-build=true
-DskipTests
```

and that's it. Simple, yes? A few things:

1. This example defaults to Docker for the image generation; you still need to have Docker installed and configured. Set the -Dquarkus.native. container-runtime=<runtime-name> option to select a different container runtime (otherwise, Docker is used as default).

2. This is still targeted at a Linux Docker image, specifically quay.io/quarkus/ubi-quarkus-native-image. So, while you can run this from the comfort of, say, a Windows development environment, the generated native artifact is still runnable inside a *nix OS only. Use the quarkus. native.builder-image property to select a different image for use.

3. You can run into memory problems (typically java. lang.OutOfMemoryError) during execution of this command. For this, be sure to set MAVEN_OPTS as an environment variable in your host machine, with ample heap space settings for the JDK. Even more fun when you realize it can fail for memory reasons, and you might not get a satisfying exception or error message indicating this specific problem.

The result will still be the same, assuming all goes well for you – you still get the native executable generated into the `target` subdirectory of your Quarkus project.

SSL Support

When your app's going native, you're going to need to be explicit about a couple of things. This is so that the native image utility bundles the dependencies necessary to support those features. One of them is SSL support. To ensure your native executable can execute HTTPS calls, you need

```
quarkus.ssl.native = true
```

Third-Party Class Support

Kudos to the Quarkus team: they've gone ahead and ported a healthy number of popular open source frameworks into Quarkus to provide native imaging support. Then there's the `@RegisterForReflection` annotation that you can add to your custom classes to make them available for AOT compilation. What about third-party classes that you have no control over and haven't been properly "Quarkused"?

When you inevitably try to use a library that doesn't expose itself for GraalVM's AOT,[7] you will need a way to manually expose that class to the native image tool. You will get some variety of the following exception at runtime, only when the application is packaged in native mode:

```
org.jboss.resteasy.spi.UnhandledException: io.smallrye.
jwt.build.JwtException: JwtProvider io.smallrye.jwt.build.
impl.JwtProviderImpl could not be instantiated: java.lang.
```

---

[7]Usually because it doesn't have a public, no-arg constructor or it uses a lot of reflection.

153

InstantiationException: Type `io.smallrye.jwt.build.impl.JwtProviderImpl` can not be instantiated reflectively as it does not have a no-parameter constructor or the no-parameter constructor has not been added explicitly to the native image

No biggie: you resolve this by manually declaring the class's layout and structure to the native image tool in GraalVM. Create a file named "reflection-config.json" in the resources directory of your Quarkus project. To address the runtime exception earlier, here's an example reflection-config.json:

```
[
    {
        "name" : "io.smallrye.jwt.build.impl.JwtProviderImpl",
        "allDeclaredConstructors" : true,
        "allPublicConstructors" : true,
        "allDeclaredMethods" : true,
        "allPublicMethods" : true,
        "allDeclaredFields" : true,
        "allPublicFields" : true
    }
]
```

OK, what's all this then? I've declared io.smallrye.jwt.build.impl.JwtProviderImpl as a class that needs AOT compilation, specifically requiring that all its constructors, public or private, all fields and all its methods, *all of them*, should be imaged by the native image tool. GraalVM will be well advised to pay attention to my declaration, for I am a powerful man![8]

---

[8]Editor's note: No you're not.

All that's left is to deliver the instruction to GraalVM at maven build time:

```
<properties>
        <quarkus.package.type>native</quarkus.package.type>
        <quarkus.native.additional-build-args>-H:Reflection
        ConfigurationFiles=reflection-config.json</quarkus.
        native.additional-build-args>
</properties>
```

-H:ReflectionConfigurationFiles is a GraalVM parameter that you use to pass the *reflection-config.json* file to the runtime; you can also set it in the application.properties file. I prefer using the POM.xml, because it keeps all the build-time configuration in one place. Now ~~dance,~~ build!

Package a Quarkus App As a Docker Image

The previous exercises were to show you how to turn your boring vanilla JVM code into a blazing fast and lightweight (Linux)OS-native bundle (Windows support is still experimental as at the time of this writing). For true WORP goodness, you should bundle the whole thing as Docker image unto itself. This is true WORP thinking, with a microservice twist: it's bundled as a functional unit, in its own little container bubble, and you get to distribute it as a single package. Yeah, that's right: we're going to package a Quarkus app as a Docker image.

Dockerfile

The Dockerfile is the instruction set for the Docker runtime for when it's creating an image. When you run the docker build command, the Docker runtime will look for a Dockerfile in the current directory; using instructions in the file, it will create a Docker image that you can publish or run. For the purposes of this demo, you'll use the Dockerfile to configure

- The operating system you want to base your Docker image on.

- File/directory sharing instructions – you need your code to pass into this image somehow.

- TCP ports to expose by default – the port on which your microservice container will expose the microservice.

- Shell commands, scripts, or programs to run immediately after the container is started.

The Quarkus maven archetype generates two kinds of Dockerfile in the /src/main/docker directory:

- Dockerfile.jvm[9] for creating a Docker image that runs your Quarkus app in JVM mode (read: traditional java application run)

- Dockerfile.native for creating a Docker image that runs your Quarkus app as a native image

Clearly, I'm in this only for native business, but the same steps apply for JVM mode images. For the remainder of this section, I'll be using the ". native" Dockerfile alone. Here's what's going on inside the native Dockerfile:

```
FROM registry.access.redhat.com/ubi8/ubi-minimal:8.1
WORKDIR /work/
COPY target/*-runner /work/application
RUN chmod 775 /work /work/application
EXPOSE 8080
CMD ["./application", "-Dquarkus.http.host=0.0.0.0"]
```

---

[9]The default filename is just "Dockerfile"; you need to use a -f flag if you need to use Dockerfile with any extension you choose. The Quarkus gang just used ". native" and ". jvm" to indicate which Dockerfile to use for native and JVM modes, respectively.

and this is what all of that means:

- **FROM** stipulates the base image, that is, an existing docker image on top of which I want to build my own image.

- **WORKDIR** defines a directory to hold transient files and data that the entire image generation process can use.

- **COPY** asks that the files ending in "-runner" in the directory "target" be moved into the /work/application directory. **Remember**: I defined /work/ in the WORKDIR directive immediately before this directive.

- **RUN** will run the specified Unix command.

- **EXPOSE** will ask that the container open up port 8080 on itself.

- **CMD** will run the defined commands when the image is launched as a container.

Don't worry if some of this feels uncomfortable – go on and read this section as many times as you like. If you'd like more formal definitions of these Dockerfile commands, check out the Dockerfile reference.

Build a Docker Image

The native Dockerfile comes with some instructions and sensible defaults. So sensible and instructional that you can take the instructions and execute them as is. So, after you've built your native executable with either `mvn package -Pnative` or the in-docker manual build, you should be able to execute

```
docker build -f src/main/docker/Dockerfile.native -t apress-
quarkus/code-with-quarkus . (3)
```

Breakdown time!

1. `build` is the command that the docker utility uses to construct an image.

2. The `-f` flag directs the docker utility to a custom-named Dockerfile (`src/main/docker/Dockerfile.native` in this case).

3. The `-t` flag tells the docker runtime what to name and tag the image. The format I'm using here is `<namespace>/<application-name>`. Pay attention to the period at the end up there; it's important. The `build` command has a tendency to choke without that being there.

and that's it. All goes well, you should have your very own docker-imaged Quarkus app. This is an image based on Native mode Quarkus. If you prefer, use `Dockerfile.jvm` for JVM mode quarkus. Verify that docker has the image stored by running `docker images` in your terminal window. what I get.

```
REPOSITORY                                   TAG
IMAGE ID              SIZE
lambci/lambda                                java11
3bc93227d833          421MB
quay.io/quarkus/centos-quarkus-maven         20.0.0-java11
39d6594a5a6a          1.86GB
quay.io/quarkus/ubi-quarkus-native-image     20.0.0-java11
91fb19e82ebc          1.43GB
lambci/lambda                                provided
81c66411cd01          698MB
quarkus/code-with-quarkus                    latest
0dc7b0de59d6          220MB
```

There I have **quarkus/code-with-quarkus** in my list of images. It means I can run my entire Quarkus app as a "black-box" application, preconfigured and contained inside a complete operating system. It also means I can distribute the app as a canned, ready to ~~drink~~ run platform, by publishing this image to the docker hub; just like you can create a Java JAR, use it locally or send it to the central maven repository.

Run a Docker Container from an Image

With the app baked as an image, you can run a container from that image with

```
docker run -i --rm -p 8081:8080 quarkus/code-with-quarkus
```

Here, I'm mapping port 8081 on my local machine to port 8080 on the running container instance. This way, when I send an HTTP request to port 8081 in my host machine's browser, the request is forwarded to my running container's port 8080, on which the code-with-quarkus app is listening for connections.

In a real-world application, there will be multiple instances of an app like code-with-quarkus, running as containers. The containers could all be running on one machine or spread out among multiple machines in a cluster formation. When we start talking about multiple instances of the same container, we need some sort of load balancer or orchestrator that will sit and distribute incoming service requests among the containers. Fundamentally, this is the promise of containers and microservices: the ability to run insular deployments of software products in a fashion that can automatically scale to a high degree of granularity. When demand for a particular microservice increases, a container orchestration layer can spawn new containers of that microservice alone to deal with the increased demand.

Docker provides Swarm as its orchestration and load balancing module. An alternative and more sophisticated orchestrator is Kubernetes, or K8s, as we cool kids call it. In the AWS cloud, you have

- Elastic Container Service (ECS)

- Elastic Kubernetes Service (EKS)

Microsoft Azure has Azure Kubernetes Service (AKS). They didn't come up with a clever name for their raw container orchestrator.

Serverless Microservices

I've been throwing "serverless" around all over this book so far, maybe even defined it. Here it is once again.

The serverless deployment of an application means simply to deploy your application without having to configure an application server or a host server. You shouldn't care about sizing the server, securing the server, and clustering, scaling, monitoring, or managing it. The actual machine, physical or virtual, that your application will be deployed to is not your problem. In most cases, you only need to provide the deployment unit (jar, .js, .java, .py, etc.) to the serverless platform provider. Quarkus provides support for the major players in the serverless/cloud space (Amazon, Microsoft, Red Hat).

Most serverless platforms are event-driven: you deploy your code in a serverless platform and your code is triggered by events within the provider's cloud ecosystem. You could have your code triggered by an HTTP request as in a vanilla web service; your code could be triggered by a database event (insert, update, delete); your code could be triggered by messages from a queueing service like SQS (from Amazon Web Services). These event connections are typically provided by your cloud provider, and you should only need to supply the code and configure the event connection.

Serverless applications are designed to be focused, efficient, and scalable. Quick in 'n' out. They're not for long-running applications. In general, you'll find that most serverless providers use the term "serverless functions" – this is important: serverless functions are treated like functional programming implementations. They're not supposed to maintain persistent state (at least not without auxiliary storage like a database or message queue); they're not made to be long-lived. Your cloud provider expects to trigger your application code with a supported event, run your code, and exit the function, preferably with a brisk response time.

Now, the perks that a specific cloud provider can provide with its serverless offering will vary from provider to provider – Microsoft, Amazon, OpenShift, and so on – all provide their own unique perks in their serverless services. On the whole though, the serverless deployment model uniquely meshes well with microservice architecture:

- Microservices being lightweight and narrowly focused by design sit well in a serverless deployment model. Think about it: "micro"service that executes a narrow function, plus serverless deployment that's lightweight and brisk in execution.

- Amazon Web Services (AWS) and Microsoft's Azure cloud platforms provide seamless versioning of serverless functions so that you can update the code, deployment after deployment, and maintain reasonable backward compatibility and contract stability with your service consumers.

- In true WORP fashion, you won't need to care about the OS, server, or cluster you're deploying your application to. The native image is packaged as a completely self-sufficient deployment unit.

Yawn. Okay, let's try Amazon Web Services serverless deployments.[10]

Amazon Web Services Serverless Deployment

Traditional Java applications aren't suited to serverless deployment. Don't take it from me; take it from the most popular cloud platform in the market:

- **Minimize your deployment package size to its runtime necessities.**

- Minimize the complexity of your dependencies. **Prefer simpler frameworks that load quickly on execution context startup.** For example, prefer simpler Java dependency injection (IoC) frameworks like Dagger or Guice over more complex ones like Spring Framework.

- **Reduce the time it takes Lambda to unpack deployment packages** authored in Java by putting your dependency `.jar` files in a separate /lib directory. This is faster than putting all your function's code in a single jar with a large number of `.class` files.

Wow, harsh. But their words, not mine. All of these basically rule out:

- Spring Boot

- A fat JAR

- Vanilla JavaEE

Quarkus is going to show them. Quarkus *is going to show them all.*

Don't worry; you won't have to wrangle "the cloud" for this demonstration. I'm going to show you how to deploy a native Quarkus application to a local simulation of Amazon's serverless platform, running

---

[10]Did you yawn too just now? I hope so! They're supposed to be infectious!

on your computer. Amazon Web Services (AWS) serverless platform is a product called **Lambda**. To deploy code to Lambda, you'll need to select what's called a "runtime".

AWS Lambda Runtimes

You have your choice of different runtimes, roughly corresponding to the programming language you're working in; so there's the PHP, JavaScript, Python, Java, and so on runtimes. Because a native image is no longer clearly bound to a programming language (at least to the OS), I'm going to opt for what AWS calls the **custom runtime.**

Package Quarkus for Lambda

The Lambda execution environment treats your code like…code. By that, I mean that it doesn't treat your Quarkus application like a stand-alone, independently deployable application. Rather, it sees it more like a java method or class that it needs to call. So in this execution context, Lambda doesn't need your Quarkus application to "start up" in the way I've been showing it: no need to start the embedded Netty app server, no need to care about ports or host IPs or the REST URL paths I've defined per the JAX-RS standards – in fact, it can't use any of the JAX-RS REST annotations I've defined. From the perspective of the AWS Lambda runtime, this is the only question that needs answering:

> *When an event message is sent to Lambda, intended for your Quarkus application, what method does Lambda need to call?*

What we need is a…

Quarkus Lambda Event Handler

Remember: Serverless applications are event-driven. The events are supplied as message payloads from other services in your cloud platform. A database action (insert, update, delete), an HTTP/S request, and a messaging queue payload are all viable event sources (among others). The actual data from these sources will be embedded inside the event payload that will be delivered to your serverless function. I'll need to define an entrypoint for events to be delivered to my Quarkus application, separate from the JAX-RS resource classes I have defined. To support Lambda event handling, I need the Quarkus Lambda plugin:

```
mvn quarkus:add-extension -Dextension=quarkus-amazon-lambda
```

Then I can add a Lambda handler class to my Quarkus project:

```
import javax.inject.Inject;
import javax.inject.Named;
import com.amazonaws.services.lambda.runtime.Context;
import com.amazonaws.services.lambda.runtime.RequestHandler;

@Named("http-lambda-handler")
public class LambdaHandlerImpl implements RequestHandler<Hello
Request,HelloResponse> (1) {

    @Inject
    ExampleResource restResource; (2)

    final Logger logger = Logger.getLogger(LambdaHandlerImpl.
    class.getName());

    @Override
    public ConversionResponse handleRequest (3)(HelloRequest
    input, Context context) {
        logger.info("Received serverless request: "+context.
        getAwsRequestId()+"; function version: "+context.
        getFunctionVersion());
        return restResource.hello(input));
    }
}
```

There's not too much going on here:

1. The AWS Java SDK provides the `RequestHandler` interface. Implementing this interface marks this class as a Lambda handler class. It is typesafe – I'm supplying the expected request and response classes as parameters. The AWS SDK will extract the core message data from the Lambda event payload and cast it into the required types. There can be only one active handler per serverless Quarkus deployment. Using the `@Named` annotation from CDI to name this Lambda handler bean class, I now need to configure the handler in application.properties:

   `quarkus.lambda.handler=http-lambda-handler`

   This tells Quarkus to mount the named bean as the Lambda event handler. You can then use profiles to set up different handlers like

   `%test.quarkus.lambda.handler=test-http-lambda-handler`.

2. Because I've baked a lot of my business logic into the `ExampleResource` JAX-RS REST resource class, I now need to inject it into this handler so I can reuse the business logic. This isn't an ideal design, so let this be a lesson to you! Encapsulate your core business logic in reusable classes and patterns like the Data Access Object (DAO) or Command patterns.

3. `handleRequest` is the method inherited from the `RequestHandler` interface. It supplies the Lambda event message payload, as well as some contextual information about the Lambda runtime and the function that was invoked.

This concludes the code changes necessary to support AWS lambda deployment. To be clear, none of this is native image deployment-specific; it's all standard Lambda stuff here.

"Monolambda" Serverless Application

Because Quarkus currently supports just one Lambda handler per app, you might be wondering what to do when you have multiple API endpoints to support via REST. This is what the so-called "monolambda" approach solves. Treat the single Lambda handler as an entrypoint or Facade for the rest of your application. From inside your handler, you are free to dispatch the Lambda event to any other part of your application. You can use any part of the context and metadata to decide on what to do with an incoming event. This is what is sometimes known as a "monolambda."

Tip   Be mindful of the Quarkus extensions, producers, and beans you define in your application. Quarkus spends some time during startup to clear unused components out of memory. This can be a couple of seconds, depending on how much clutter there is in your application. You can control this behavior by setting the `quarkus.arc.remove-unused-beans` to none or `false`. `framework` is also an option so that only non-custom beans are removed.

To deploy your Quarkus project to Lambda, AWS mandates the following:

1. The deployment unit must be named "bootstrap", if it is going to be using the custom runtime (i.e., a native image).

2. The deployment unit must be packaged as a zip file. You can also use a JAR if you're deploying your app in JVM mode.

3. The deployment unit can be packaged with what is called a Serverless Application Model (SAM) file, in YAML format. This file provides crucial deploy-time metadata about your serverless application to the Lambda platform.

4. A LAMBDA_ROLE_ARN environment variable that corresponds to the lambda execution role that you have created in the Identity Access Manager, in the AWS console. For the purposes of this book, you can ignore this step – all of the samples here are locally executable.

When you add the quarkus-amazon-lambda extension to your project and build it with mvn package, Quarkus automatically

- Creates two files named sam.jvm.yaml and sam.native.yaml.

- Creates manage.sh and bootstrap-example.sh files containing helpful shell scripting functions for deploying and running your application in AWS Lambda.

- Creates a "function.zip" file that is supposed to be the complete deployable kit. You should be able to straight up upload this file to Amazon's S3 service and point a Lambda function at it.

What your *function.zip* contains depends on the compilation mode; what you'll get inside for a JVM mode app is different for a native image app. The JVM mode kit is not interesting (or recommended) for serverless deployment, so I won't go into detail about it. No, I'm here for that native business.

AWS requires that custom runtime serverless projects be supplied to lambda

- With the executable named "bootstrap"

- And bootstrap be delivered in a zip file named *function.zip*

And that's what `quarkus-amazon-lambda` does. It will rename your deployable output to *bootstrap* and then add it to a *function.zip* file; the output being in the target directory. Additionally, you'll find the utility shell scripts, *sam.jvm.yaml* and *sam.native.yaml* in the same directory. Let's check it out.

AWS Serverless Application Model

This is the piece de resistance to all of this. The Serverless Application Model (SAM) is a framework that AWS provides for defining metadata for a serverless application. It's mostly defined in a YAML file and consumed by different AWS tools to provision a serverless application. I'm not going to go into too much detail of the model – the whole thing is a robust schema of options. Instead, I'll show you only what you need to know to get a simple Quarkus serverless deployment going. Here's some SAM file content you can use:

```
AWSTemplateFormatVersion: '2010-09-09'
Transform: AWS::Serverless-2016-10-31
Description: AWS Serverless Quarkus - com.apress.
samples::lambda
Globals:
  Api:
```

```
BinaryMediaTypes:
 - "*/*"

Resources:
  LambdaNativeFunction:
    Type: AWS::Serverless::Function
    Properties:
      Handler: not.needed.for.provided.runtime
      Runtime: provided
      CodeUri: target/function.zip
      MemorySize: 128
      Policies: AWSLambdaBasicExecutionRole
      Timeout: 15
        ProvisionedConcurrencyConfig:
        ProvisionedConcurrentExecutions: 5:
      Environment:
        Variables:
          DISABLE_SIGNAL_HANDLERS: true
```

A lot of this is boilerplate stuff that won't vary too much from deployment to deployment; I've highlighted the salient bits:

1. **Handler**: If this were a JVM mode serverless deployment, I would have io.quarkus.amazon. lambda.runtime.QuarkusStreamHandler::hand leRequest in there instead of the dummy text I've placed there. The QuarkusStreamHandler class (and the handleRequest method in that class) is a dedicated Quarkus-provided class that's required for AWS serverless deployment. For the native deployment scenario, any string will do. The field is mandatory, per AWS.

2. **Runtime**: This is where I would ordinarily specify "java8" or "java11", were this a JVM mode package. Native mode packaging requires the "provided" runtime, a.k.a. custom runtime.

3. **CodeUri**: The path to the deployment package. This tells SAM where to find the deployment package/ code to load for a serverless deployment. Since my deployment package is in the /target subdirectory of the Quarkus project, that's what I've configured here. In a real AWS deployment, you would supply a path to an Amazon S3 bucket where you would have previously uploaded the zip file containing your Quarkus app.

4. **MemorySize**: What's the maximum amount of RAM I'd like AWS to allocate to my serverless app?

5. **ProvisionedConcurrencyConfig**: This defines the minimum amount of concurrent instances of this Lambda I'd like to run. When you think of Lambdas as threads, this option defines how many Lambda instances should be pooled and ready to serve requests. It's a great choice for minimizing latency or variability in the latency. This is what AWS calls "Provisioned Concurrency." This helps you blunt the effects of Lambda cold starts. The downside is that you'll now always be paying for those lambdas, whether or not they're running. Note that this isn't a requirement – you can run a perfectly fine Lambda function without this feature. I'm including it here only for completeness, because AWS just introduced this feature last December (2019).

6. **Environment**: This section of the SAM template defines environment variables that I expect the Lambda runtime to load into whatever OS it's using. These variables are also available for consumption by my code. Here, I've defined only the DISABLE_SIGNAL_HANDLERS variable as recommended by the Quarkus team. Disabling signal handlers means that the native image will not respond to OS-level instructions like SIGKILL and SIGABRT.

I simply save this template into a YAML file named **sam.native.yaml** and go about my business. Finally, I can choose to now deploy my app either to the AWS cloud or run it locally in a simulated Lambda runtime. I'll take #2 please; otherwise, you'll need to go sign up for an AWS account and configure stuff, which is out of the scope of this fine book. To the simulated environment!

AWS SAM CLI Deployment

With my Quarkus application outfitted for serverless deployment for the AWS Lambda platform, I have the choice of uploading my kit named "function.zip" to the AWS online console. I could also just bring the Lambda platform to my local machine for a simulated deployment.

The SAM command-line interface (CLI) is a portable serverless application toolkit provided by AWS. Use it to test, deploy, and manage your serverless applications both locally and in the AWS cloud.[11] It's packaged as a Docker image (of course); you already have Docker Desktop installed by now, don't you? Download and install the CLI for your operating system and let's crack on!

---

[11]And also check out Localstack to replicate a lot of services and functions of the AWS cloud, right on your local machine!

Once your installation is complete, you should be able to run the following command in a terminal window and get results:

```
sam --version
```

With a correctly packaged serverless Quarkus application, the SAM CLI will load and deploy my application, using the SAM template I supply.

It'll use the *sam.native.yaml* file as the definition to launch the app. I now need to trigger my app, simulating an actual Lambda event as it would be triggered in the AWS cloud. Use the generate-event command to use the SAM CLI to generate sample payloads for different AWS services. Observe

```
sam local generate-event apigateway aws-proxy
```

Running the preceding command will generate a sample JSON document that represents what will be passed to your Lambda by AWS's API Gateway service. API Gateway is a service that you can use as the front facing entrypoint to your microservice. Think of it like a web server provided by Amazon. Here's a trimmed down version of the generated document:

```
{
  "body": "This is the HTTP request body",
  "resource": "/{proxy+}",
  "path": "/path/to/resource",
  "httpMethod": "POST",
  "isBase64Encoded": true,
  "queryStringParameters": {
    "foo": "bar"
  },
```

```
"multiValueQueryStringParameters": {
  "foo": [
    "bar"
  ]
},
"pathParameters": {
  "proxy": "/path/to/resource"
},
"headers": {
  "Accept": "text/html,application/xhtml+xml,application/
  xml;q=0.9,image/webp,*/*;q=0.8",
  "Accept-Encoding": "gzip, deflate, sdch",
  "Accept-Language": "en-US,en;q=0.8",
  "Cache-Control": "max-age=0",
  "Host": "1234567890.execute-api.us-east-1.amazonaws.com"
},
"multiValueHeaders": {
  "Accept": [
    "text/html,application/xhtml+xml,application/
    xml;q=0.9,image/webp,*/*;q=0.8"
  ],
  "Accept-Encoding": [
    "gzip, deflate, sdch"
  ],
  "Accept-Language": [
    "en-US,en;q=0.8"
  ],
  "Cache-Control": [
    "max-age=0"
  ]
},
```

```
"requestContext": {
    "accountId": "123456789012",
    "resourceId": "123456",
    "stage": "prod",
    "requestId": "c6af9ac6-7b61-11e6-9a41-93e8deadbeef",
    "requestTime": "09/Apr/2015:12:34:56 +0000",
    "requestTimeEpoch": 1428582896000,
    "path": "/prod/path/to/resource",
    "resourcePath": "/{proxy+}",
    "httpMethod": "POST",
    "apiId": "1234567890",
    "protocol": "HTTP/1.1"
  }
}
```

The generated JSON document shown here is a sample representing a Lambda event coming from the API Gateway service. API Gateway is another AWS service that you can use to provide HTTP/S interfaces to applications deployed in AWS. This whole document is then converted into a Java object and delivered to your code by the Lambda runtime. I'll save this sample as a file named *payload.json*. All that's left to do is to invoke my Lambda-packaged application using payload.json as the event. For that, I'll run the following command from within my Quarkus project folder:

```
sam local invoke -t sam.native.yaml --event payload.json
```

Here's what I'm doing with this command:

1. sam local invoke executes a local invocation of the serverless application that's...

2.   ...defined in **sam.native.yaml**. The -t flag loads the
      file for the SAM cli. If I wanted to deploy my app in JVM
      mode, I'd use the generated *sam.jvm.yaml* instead.

3.   The –event flag loads the JSON payload from the
      file named payload.json, using it as the request
      event payload to pass to my lambda function. This
      effectively treats this interaction like a REST service
      request. I have access to a lot of metadata in this
      event, so I could add conditional logic to inspect the
      URL or HTTP method that was invoked to generate
      this event.

Here's the result of my command execution:

```
[START RequestId: 4de58426-2477-1dc6-72f2-b5f4dc42b611 Version:
$LATEST]
{"timestamp":"2020-04-12T12:49:56.99Z","sequence":633,
"loggerClassName":"org.jboss.slf4j.
JBossLoggerAdapter","loggerName":"com.apress.samples.handlers.
LambdaHandlerImpl","level":"INFO",
"message":"Received serverless request: 4de58426-2477-1dc6-
72f2-b5f4dc42b611; function version:
$LATEST","threadName":"Lambda Thread","threadId":15,"mdc":{},
"ndc":"","hostName":"4241f4c86237","processName":
"NativeImageGeneratorRunner$JDK9Plus","processId":488}
[END RequestId: 4de58426-2477-1dc6-72f2-b5f4dc42b611]
[REPORT RequestId: 4de58426-2477-1dc6-72f2-b5f4dc42b611
Init Duration: 799.91 ms         Duration: 17.88 ms
    Billed Duration: 100 ms Memory Size: 128 MB      Max Memory
    Used: 58 MB]

{"responsContent":"Hello Quarkus Person, Welcome to AWS
Lambda!"}
```

This run of this command shows me a couple of things that are specifically provided by the Lambda runtime:

1. I can see the running version of my Lambda app as **$LATEST**, because I didn't deliberately configure a version number.

2. I can see how long it took for the Lambda runtime to start up,[12] **"Init Duration"** – 799.91ms.

3. It shows me how long my serverless function took to completely execute, **"Duration"** – 17.88ms.

4. I can then see how much time I would be billed for, **"Billed Duration"** (were these running in the AWS cloud and not in my local machine) – 100ms. How come? The minimum billable duration in AWS is 100ms, regardless of how much less time your serverless function runs for.

5. I see the maximum amount of RAM my app consumed at any point during its execution, "Max Memory Used" – 58MB.

And that, ladies and gents, is how you deploy an AWS Lambda function in your local development environment. You can use the SAM CLI to deploy your lambda to an actual AWS environment as well; you just need to register for a free AWS account. Get a more comprehensive introduction to SAM starting with the wonderful AWS documentation (seriously, Oracle and AWS write some killer docs).

---

[12]This is a little bit of a sore spot with serverless functions with any cloud provider: the very first invocation of a function tends to be costly as the infrastructure warms up to serve your code. AWS doesn't bill for this cold start time, but it still sucks for the unlucky first user. The Provisioned Concurrency setting was introduced to address this issue.

The model of deployment I've just walked through is the most flexible. My serverless Quarkus application can field events from any other AWS component – databases, message queues, CloudWatch, or anything. My application doesn't expose an HTTP endpoint, but it is kitted out for flexibility. If I want to deploy my Lambda as a RESTful web application, complete with a REST endpoint that can be hit with HTTP, I'm going to need to get *funky*. Cue the bass!

Funqy Serverless Apps

Funqy – not a typo – is an effort by the Quarkus team to standardize the deployment of serverless functions. With Funqy, you can write a REST resource once, and Quarkus can make it readily deployable for multiple different serverless platforms and deployment scenarios. So with code like

```
@Funq("generate-anagram")
public AnagramResponse getAnagram(AnagramRequest request) {
    ...
}
```

@Funq marks this method as a "function". From this point, the only question I need to answer is "what platform do I want to deploy this function to?". Here are some answers:

- AWS Lambda? I just add the quarkus-funqy-amazon-lambda extension to expose getAnagram as a Lambda function. Additionally, I'll configure quarkus.funqy. export=generate-anagram. Funqy and the Quarkus lambda extension will work to manage the handler for receiving and unmarshalling Lambda events. You still get just one @Funq per deployable however.

- Azure Function? I'll need the `quarkus-azure-functions-http` extension. The nice bit of this extension is that it allows me to expose multiple `@Funq`-decorated methods as proper REST endpoints, complete with URL and all.

Funqy is still under development at this time of this writing, but watch this space! It's an exciting direction for the platform as a whole.

AWS Serverless Success with Quarkus

If deploying your code serverlessly feels a little strange to you, it's completely normal and you're not alone. It requires a mindset shift that might take some time. In addition to all that I've already talked about here, bear these in mind:

- There's a default 5-minute limit imposed on Lambda functions in AWS. This means that whatever you do, your serverless app must complete its processing within that time limit. This is not ideal for batch processes, so be careful what you try to execute in a lambda.

- Static variables, class-level variables, and singletons are reused between invocations of a lambda function. So, get really cozy with the `@ApplicationScoped` and `@Singleton` annotations as there could be some serious savings there.

- If you're caching data *inside* your function (instead of inside an externally managed cache), know that that cache is isolated to that instance of your function. AWS supports up to 1000 concurrent invocations of the same Lambda function. There's no guarantee that the same instance of your function will be invoked successively enough to make an internal cache worth it.

- If you're caching data inside your function, you're spending RAM. Take that into account when sizing the RAM usage of your function with your *sam.yaml* file. Sure a bunch of Strings won't cost too much,[13] but if you're caching large objects like media content, size appropriately.

- Consider using AWS's Simple Storage Service (S3) to persist data between Lambda invocations. S3 offers cheap replication, security, accelerated delivery, and durability which could help in certain storage and caching scenarios.

- Brand new from AWS is the Elastic File System. When I learned about this, I was shaking with excitement. It's a File System for Lambda functions that's shared between concurrent invocations of a Lambda function, with locking and multi-availability zone access. This is poised to be a game changer for managing state, data, and configuration for Lambdas.

- Avoid or minimize recursive invocations inside your function code. Unchecked recursion will not only cost you more financially – each invocation of Lambda is billed – your function could simply just choke out on memory as well.

- Treat your lambda function exactly like a function: don't hold mutable state in it. Your function could be invoked once or possibly multiple times for the same request.

---

[13]The new-ish Compact Strings feature in the JVM certainly won't hurt!

CHAPTER 5

Quarkus Data Access

I'll admit, I was *one of them*. I was a data access purist: I like my DAOs chilled, my PreparedStatements prepared, and my SQL handwritten with the care and tenderness of a lover. The world moved on to Hibernate, Java Persistence API (JPA), and everything in between; I clung to my "SQL IS THE LAW" doctrine. Then came Spring Boot Data JPA. And *even then* I relished in making my own life difficult. Not for nothing though, I still believe in raw SQL – a well-crafted SQL statement will outperform Object-Relational Mapping (ORM).

The fact is that ORM frameworks are a massive time saver and wonderful for many use cases. Quarkus provides *a lot* of data access support, not just SQL. In addition to SQL-based storage, Quarkus provides extensions to access

- NoSQL storage like MongoDB and DynamoDB

- Message brokers like Kafka and AMQP

- Plain Java Messaging Service (JMS) brokers like RabbitMQ and ActiveMQ

In addition to the standard data access that you ought to expect from any production-grade microservice framework, Quarkus sweetens the deal with

- **Panache**: Say what you will about the Quarkus framework, but the authors know how to name a product! Panache is a collection of augmentations that Quarkus adds to standard ORM structures, aimed at reducing the amount of code you need to write. If you're familiar with the Active Record pattern, that's about the gist of it.

- **Reactive SQL**: A CPU-efficient, event-driven approach to dealing with results from a database query. Exquisite.

I'll start with the fundamentals before we get to the good stuff.

SQL Data Sources

Obviously, the first thing to attend to is to configure the databases you're going to be interacting with. This is the story of configuring and managing SQL data sources in Quarkus. Out of the box, Quarkus has extension support for the following databases:

- MySQL: Add the `jdbc-mysql` extension.

- MSSQL: Add the `jdbc-mssql` extension.

- PostgreSQL: Add the `jdbc-postgresql` extension.

- Embedded databases – H2, MariaDB, and Derby: Add the `jdbc-h2`, `jdbc-mariadb`, and `jdbc-derby` extensions, respectively.

- "Other"

"Other" refers to support for the uncool databases. Nah, I'm just kidding – it's support for any database that doesn't have a packaged Quarkus extension. For the named databases in the preceding list, Quarkus has repackaged their drivers for native mode compatibility. So you're still free to configure a JDBC connection with the following properties, for example:

```
quarkus.datasource.db-kind=other
quarkus.datasource.jdbc.driver=oracle.jdbc.driver.OracleDriver
quarkus.datasource.jdbc.url=jdbc:oracle:thin:@<ip>:<port>/ORCL_SVC
quarkus.datasource.username=scott
quarkus.datasource.password=tiger
```

Your Oracle database will be accessible with this config. Just don't count on native mode compatibility – JVM mode only. For the Quarkus-packaged support, just configure the proper quarkus.datasource.db-kind and provide the JDBC URL:

```
quarkus.datasource.db-kind=postgresql
quarkus.datasource.jdbc.url=jdbc:postgresql://localhost:5432/
anagrams
quarkus.datasource.username=scottus
quarkus.datasource.password=tigerus
```

This config will load the correct JDBC driver and guarantee correct functioning in a native mode deployment. Why stop at one? You can throw in more data sources in there by **naming** the data sources. Observe:

```
#anagram players data source
quarkus.datasource.players.db-kind=postgresql
quarkus.datasource.players.jdbc.url=jdbc:postgresql:
//localhost:5432/anagrams
quarkus.datasource.players.username=scottus
quarkus.datasource.players.password=tigerus
#anagram metrics data source
```

```
quarkus.datasource.metrics.db-kind=mysql
quarkus.datasource.metrics.jdbc.url=jdbc:mysql:
//localhost:3306/anagrams
quarkus.datasource.metrics.username=not-scottus
quarkus.datasource.metrics.password=not-tigerus
```

With the **name** I've introduced in the standard JDBC connection properties, I can configure as many different data sources as I like in the same application. Obviously, you'll need to install PostgreSQL or any supported database of your choice. Download an installer from www.postgresql.org/download/. If you're cool and *hip* like the kids say I am,[1] you could skip all that and just run the following docker command. Courtesy of the Quarkus official documentation:

```
docker run --ulimit memlock=-1:-1 -it --rm=true
--memory-swappiness=0 --name postgres-quarkus-hibernate
-e POSTGRES_USER=scottus -e POSTGRES_PASSWORD=tigerus
-e POSTGRES_DB=anagrams -p 5432:5432 postgres:10.5
```

The preceding docker command will

1. Pull the official PostgreSQL version 10.5 image into your local machine

2. Configure it with the username and password passed to POSTGRES_USER and POSTGRES_ PASSWORD environment variables

3. Create a database passed to POSTGRES_DB

4. Map port 5432 on your local machine to port 5432 in your PostgreSQL docker container

All in one move. Smooth.

---

[1] Editor's note: No one under the age of 75 considers you "cool."

Configure a JDBC Connection Pool Manager

Rule of thumb: You *need* a connection pool in your life. You shouldn't deploy anything production-grade without using a connection pool and, hence, a connection pool manager. A connection pool is any configured number of resource connections that are pre-created and kept in memory. The idea is that whenever client code needs access to that resource, the running code just picks up a warm connection and goes. In general, creating connections of any kind tends to be expensive and time-consuming. Pooling those connections ahead of time translates into significant latency improvements and even throughput gains.

The connection pool manager you select for your application makes a lot of difference – they're not all the same. The pool manager is responsible for creating, maintaining, and retiring the connections in the pool. The Quarkus squad chose Agroal over Hikari as the default connection pool manager. Based on their testing, Agroal provides the high level of efficient pool management befitting the Supersonic Subatomic tagline; it also provides a great degree of flexibility and tunability. Add the [agroal] Quarkus extension to introduce it to your kit. You can tweak your connection pool settings with the following properties:

Property	Description
quarkus.datasource.jdbc. initial-size	How many connections should the connection pool start out with? Too many would be wasteful and eventually be a resource drag. To few and you might as well not have a connection pool at all.
quarkus.datasource.jdbc. min-size	After the pool has been started, how many connections should be maintained at any point?
quarkus.datasource.jdbc. max-size	What's the most number of connections to be held in the pool at any point?

(continued)

Property	Description
quarkus.datasource.jdbc. acquisition-timeout	How long should the connection pool manager wait to acquire a connection?
quarkus.datasource.jdbc. background-validation-interval	At what interval should the connection pool manager validate the connections in the pool? Validation is the act of checking that a connection is viable and active.
quarkus.datasource.jdbc. validation-query-sql	An SQL query that the connection manager can use to validate that the database is simple. Literally, a simple query you can guarantee to always return a result to indicate things are going well.
quarkus.datasource.jdbc. leak-detection-interval	At what interval are we checking for leaks in the connections in the pool?

These properties also can be named to support multiple data sources. The interval properties have a bit of a twist to them. They're based on the new-ish Duration class. So, to set `quarkus.datasource.jdbc.acquisition-timeout` to 2 seconds, for example, it would be

`quarkus.datasource.jdbc.acquisition-timeout = P2S`

I know, it's a bit of an acquired taste.

Is Your Data Source Healthy?

This is a really neat feature that ships with the Agroal extension. Together with the `quarkus-smallrye-health` extension, it displays database health check information at `<host:port>/health, <host:port>/health/ready` Figure 5-1 shows what the response from the health check endpoint looks like.

```
status:              "DOWN"
▼ checks:
   ▼ 0:
      name:          "Database connections health check"
      status:        "DOWN"
      ▼ data:
         ▼ default:  "Unable to execute the validation check for the default DataSource: FATAL: password authentication failed for user
                     \"postgres\""
   ▼ 1:
      name:          "diskSpaceCheck"
      status:        "UP"
      ▼ data:
         arbitraryData:  "arbitraryValue"
```

Figure 5-1. *The response from my custom health check metric*

You can disable this endpoint with the quarkus.datasource.health.
enabled property set to false. This becomes important as you'll see.

This is all well and good, but there are some scenarios in which the data source health check can be even more useful. One gripe I have with Quarkus is this: a broken database connection will not stop your Quarkus app from starting up.[2] In general, I don't want my application to start up if critical dependencies aren't healthy. If you want to do something about it though, here's how:

```
import org.eclipse.microprofile.health.HealthCheckResponse;
import org.eclipse.microprofile.health.Readiness;
import org.eclipse.microprofile.health.HealthCheckResponse.
State;

import io.quarkus.agroal.runtime.health.DataSourceHealthCheck;
import io.quarkus.runtime.StartupEvent;

public class StartupConfigCheck {
    Logger logger = Logger.getLogger(StartupConfigCheck.class.
    getName());
```

---

[2]It's probably for a good reason though – Quarkus is all about lazy loading wherever practical.

```
@Inject
@Readiness
DataSourceHealthCheck dbHealthCheck; (1)

public void failIfDBisBroken(@Observes StartupEvent (2)
startup){
    HealthCheckResponse healthCheckResponse =
    dbHealthCheck.call(); (3)
    if(healthCheckResponse.getState().equals(State.DOWN)) (4){
        logger.warning("Aborting startup: "+healthCheck
        Response.getName()+"; message: "+healthCheck
        Response.getData());
        throw new IllegalStateException("Datasource
        connection is broken; Aborting startup");
    }
}
}
```

This bean will stop a Quarkus application from starting up, if the given data source isn't available. It also provides a nice, readable message of your choosing and the freedom to execute custom logic if you like. How does it work?

1. I inject an instance of io.quarkus.agroal.runtime.
    health.DataSourceHealthCheck, the health check
    class that Agroal provides. @Readiness is there to
    reduce the chances of CDI injection errors due
    to ambiguity with any other health check class
    available.

2. I use the Quarkus lifecycle event class StartupEvent
    to be notified when the application is starting.

3. Using the health check class, I run the health check myself and obtain a HealthCheckResponse.

4. I can then interrogate the HealthCheckResponse object for the status of the health check and a bunch of useful information. If the status is "DOWN", I throw an exception with my desired message. The exception will terminate any startup in progress, saving any runtime embarrassment.

This is how I can save myself from any runtime embarrassment due to misconfiguration.

Caution   This isn't an officially documented feature of Quarkus. It's possible, though unlikely, that the bean that enables this is removed without warning in future releases.

Using SQL Data Sources

I've configured an SQL database; now to use the darn thing.

The basic JDBC access is available like so:

```
@Inject
AgroalDataSource dataSource;

public void generateAndSaveAnagram(String source){
    ...
    try(Connection connection = dataSource.getConnection()){
        PreparedStatement statement = connection.
        prepareStatement("insert into anagrams
        (anagram_text,anagram_source_id) values(?,?)");
```

```
      statement.setString(1,response.getConversionResponse());
       ResultSet results = statement.executeQuery();
   }
   ...
}
```

You only need to inject the AgroalDataSource and you can get a connection off it and follow JDBC semantics from there. Life's since gotten easier, with ORM. When you have named data sources, use @DataSource to qualify it:

```
@Inject
@DataSource("users")
AgroalDataSource dataSource;

public void insertAnagram(ConversionResponse response){
    ...
}
```

With @DataSource, I can inject the specific data source named "users". Now, shall we try some ORM on for size?

With Object-Relational Mapping

If you're an old fuddy duddy like I am, you're still a fan of artisanal, responsibly sourced, fair-trade SQL. Then there's Object-Relational Mapping (ORM) that will save you a bunch of time. IF you're already comfortable with the principles of ORM, you can skip this bit and GOTO the Spring Data JPA section; else, IF you're familiar with that too, GOTO the Panache! bit. Otherwise, here's a quick primer on ORM.

The fundamental purpose of ORM is to abstract the database layer away behind Java classes. Java classes for everything. Ideally, you'll never have to deal with raw or vendor-specific SQL anymore. Instead of manually querying the database, picking off results from the ResultSet and then possibly constructing a value object, you use an ORM layer.

An ORM layer will have you pre-create entity classes that map to database tables; the fields of that class map to the table columns. This way, you interact with the database only in object-oriented terms – the ORM layer handles everything else like transactions, sequence number generation, paginating and sorting results, and all the CRUD business. There are two major players in this space:

- Hibernate: Use the quarkus-hibernate-orm extension.

- Java Persistence API (JPA).

The Java Persistence API is a specification from JavaEE that defines components, behaviors, and annotations that make up an ORM layer. The specification is then adopted and implemented by vendors like Eclipse.

It used to be that Hibernate had only its own set of annotations and components. Hibernate then implemented the JPA specification, so now, it's more common to have JPA-looking classes used with the Hibernate engine. I'm not going to explore either JPA or Hibernate separately – that's out of the scope of this book – rather, I'll show you how well they both gel.

It all starts with an *entity*:

```
import javax.persistence.*;

@Entity (1)
public class Anagram{

    @Id      (2)
    @GeneratedValue(strategy = GenerationType.IDENTITY,
    generator = "anagram_source_id_seq")
```

```
    @Column(name = "anagram_id",nullable = false) (3)
    private Long id;

    private String source;

    @ManyToOne(fetch = FetchType.LAZY) (4)
    @JoinColumn(name = "anagram_source_id") (5)
    AnagramSource anagramSource;
        //getters and setters
 }
...
@Entity
@Table(name = "anagram_source")
public class AnagramSource{
    @Id
    @GeneratedValue(strategy = GenerationType.IDENTITY,
    generator="")
    private Long id;

    @Column(name = "anagram_source_text", unique = true,
    nullable = false)
    private String value;

    private String anagramSourceText;

    @OneToMany(mappedBy = "anagramSource",fetch = FetchType.
    LAZY) (6)
    List<Anagram> anagrams = new ArrayList<>();
}
```

What *is* all this?

1. @Entity marks this class as a unit that Hibernate should manage. Typically, Hibernate will automatically match class name to the database table name. You can still specify the table name with the @Table annotation if you have specific naming requirements for your tables. Otherwise, Hibernate can infer the table name from the class name.

2. The @Id annotation marks this field as the primary key for this entity class. It will map this field to whatever the primary key column on the database table is. @GeneratedValue bootstraps a default key generation mechanism (or sequence). Hibernate will thus use the existing sequence on my table to handle the generation of the next ID to use for an insert. At least, that is how it's supposed to work. There's some hibernate weirdness I experienced here:

   a) Ideally, you should be able to set strategy to AUTO and Hibernate will pick up on the sequence that I configured for the ID column. This is not what happened for me. Due to an inconsistency between Hibernate and PostgreSQL, what I got instead were negative numbers in the ID column. This is not the case with MySQL based on my testing.

   b) I had to set strategy to IDENTITY and then provide the name of the PostgreSQL sequence in the generator attribute. To be clear, this is because of a disconnect between Hibernate and PostgreSQL, not a Quarkus thing.

3. @Column specifically maps this field on this class, to the database table column in the name attribute.

4. @ManyToOne designates this field as one to be used to establish a many-to-one join to a different table and its associated entity. The fetchType attribute stipulates whether this field should be populated with the related entity instance immediately or only when that field is called for. @JoinColumn will designate that field as a join field. From this, it will look up the referenced class and use the @Id column in that class as a primary key. It therefore automatically establishes a foreign key-primary key relationship between the two classes. This in turn lets Hibernate supply instances of the linked class as entities loaded from the corresponding database table:

   a) FetchType is set to LAZY here as well, for pretty much the same reasons. Also it helps to watch out for the famous N+1 problem in SQL, where one executes an additional query to retrieve data that could have been retrieved in an earlier query.

5. @OneToMany helps to establish the other end of the relationship. AnagramSource will have many Anagrams. Here, I definitely don't want all associated Anagrams eagerly loaded every time I pull the AnagramSource – for complex or large objects, that could be a long-running query. The JPA spec has some more sophisticated componentry to handle complex table relationships; check them out.

At this point, all I have is the vehicle to extract data from my PostgreSQL database. A value object. What I need now are the actual CRUD[3] components. If you're already familiar with Hibernate, rejoice! You can just start using everything you're already used to: the EntityManager, SessionFactory, Session, and .hbm.xml file (eww), all of these are welcome in Quarkus.

If you're *not* familiar with either raw Hibernate or raw JPA, well hello there! Today's your lucky day, bud: you get to see how easy it can be to pull data with Hibernate and JPA together, courtesy of our old "friend," Spring. Learning ORM with Hibernate + JPA together is a great start that will help you get a production-grade application going very quickly.

Tip   Both Eclipse and IntelliJ provide JPA entity generation plugins. With their respective plugins, you can generate entity classes from an existing SQL database.

Configure Database Loading

Hibernate on its own brings a bunch of convenience with it, especially when we take Quarkus' dev mode into account. Observe: Quarkus provides a quarkus.hibernate-orm.database.generation property, courtesy of Hibernate. There are five supported options for this property:

- create: On Quarkus startup, Hibernate will drop tables and then create them.

- validate: Hibernate will validate that the underlying database schema matches the expectations of the Java-side entity classes. It'll throw an exception otherwise.

---

[3]Create, **R**ead, **U**pdate, and **D**elete.

- drop-and-create: On startup, your Quarkus app will drop and recreate an entire database.

- update: On startup, your Quarkus app will perform an update on an existing database, using the entity classes as a reference. If the database tables have deviated from what the entity classes represent, the update will be performed.

- no-file: On startup, your Quarkus app will do nothing.

All you need to do is place a file named import.sql inside the resources directory of your application. This file should contain the insert or update statements that you want to populate the database with. How does Hibernate know anything about the structure of your database? Your entity classes. Hibernate will use all your @Entity classes to create your database structure on the fly; then it uses the contents of your import.sql to seed the database with data. When you combine this with the live reloading feature of Quarkus in dev mode, your development process becomes buttery smooth. Think about it: make changes to resources/import.sql, the changes are executed, and you go on with your engineering without having to pause and restart anything. Sweet! Here's the schema I'm working with:

```
DROP DATABASE anagrams;

CREATE DATABASE anagrams WITH TEMPLATE = template0 ENCODING =
'UTF8' LC_COLLATE = 'English_United States.1252' LC_CTYPE =
'English_United States.1252';

ALTER DATABASE anagrams OWNER TO postgres;

SET statement_timeout = 0;
SET lock_timeout = 0;
SET idle_in_transaction_session_timeout = 0;
SET client_encoding = 'UTF8';
SET standard_conforming_strings = on;
```

```
SET check_function_bodies = false;
SET xmloption = content;
SET client_min_messages = warning;
SET row_security = off;
SET default_tablespace = '';
SET default_table_access_method = heap;

CREATE TABLE anagram (
    anagram_text character varying(100) NOT NULL,
    anagram_source_id bigint NOT NULL,
    anagram_id bigint NOT NULL
);

ALTER TABLE anagram OWNER TO postgres;

CREATE SEQUENCE anagram_anagram_id_seq
    START WITH 1
    INCREMENT BY 1
    NO MINVALUE
    NO MAXVALUE
    CACHE 1;

ALTER TABLE anagram_anagram_id_seq OWNER TO postgres;

ALTER SEQUENCE anagram_anagram_id_seq OWNED BY anagram.anagram_id;

CREATE TABLE anagram_source (
    id bigint NOT NULL,
    anagram_source_text character varying NOT NULL
);

ALTER TABLE public.anagram_source OWNER TO postgres;

CREATE SEQUENCE anagram_source_id_seq
    START WITH 1
    INCREMENT BY 1
```

```
     NO MINVALUE
     NO MAXVALUE
     CACHE 1;
```

ALTER TABLE anagram_source_id_seq OWNER TO postgres;

ALTER SEQUENCE anagram_source_id_seq OWNED BY anagram_source.id;

ALTER TABLE ONLY anagram ALTER COLUMN anagram_id SET DEFAULT
nextval('anagram_anagram_id_seq'::regclass);

ALTER TABLE ONLY anagram_source ALTER COLUMN id SET DEFAULT
nextval('anagram_source_id_seq'::regclass);

ALTER TABLE ONLY anagram_source
     ADD CONSTRAINT anagram_source_pkey PRIMARY KEY (id);

ALTER TABLE ONLY anagram
     ADD CONSTRAINT unique_anagram UNIQUE (anagram_text) INCLUDE
(anagram_source_id);

CREATE INDEX fki_anagram_source_fk ON anagram USING btree
(anagram_source_id);

ALTER TABLE ONLY anagram
     ADD CONSTRAINT anagram_source_fk FOREIGN KEY (anagram_
source_id) REFERENCES anagram_source(id) NOT VALID;

Put that in your import.sql and let's roll!

With Spring Data JPA

Spring Data JPA is data access the way God intended; and it's all here in
Quarkus as well. It boils down to **extending** one of the repository (or DAO[4])
interfaces supplied by Spring Data. For now, feast your eyes and code on:

---

[4]**D**ata **A**ccess **O**bject.

- `org.springframework.data.repository.Repository`

- `org.springframework.data.repository.`
  `CrudRepository`

- `org.springframework.data.repository.`
  `JpaRepository`

- `org.springframework.data.repository.`
  `PagingAndSortingRepository`

First, add the `spring-data-jpa` extension. Following that, all you need to do is **extend** one of those interfaces and *a lot* is taken care of behind the scenes. A simple implementation:

```
import org.springframework.data.jpa.repository.JpaRepository;

public interface AnagramRepository extends
CrudRepository<Anagram,Long> (1) {
    public Anagram findByAnagramText(String anagramText); (2)
}
```

1. I extend CrudRepository with the entity type I'm looking to CRUD, plus the primary key type. This simple act grants my code a lot of power implicitly. I'll show you what I mean shortly.

2. This method definition is a stub I plan to use for, well, searching anagrams by their strings. Don't worry about the implementation for now – and forever.

I can now...use the interface as is?

That's it. It's basically magic. The CrudRepository interface – which all the other *Repository interfaces extend from – looks like this:

```
public interface CrudRepository<T, ID> extends Repository<T, ID> {

    <S extends T> S save(S entity);

    Optional<T> findById(ID primaryKey);

    Iterable<T> findAll();

    long count();

    void delete(T entity);

    boolean existsById(ID primaryKey);
...
}
```

Those methods do exactly what they're named for. Spring Boot – and Quarkus by extension – has a lot of plumbing in place so that this interface and any other that extends it is plug-n-play. So, by default, you get all the CRUD operations for free. It gets even better: the findByAnagramText method works without me having to implement the method in a class. This is possible because Spring Boot can infer what kind of query I'm trying to execute, given a string value that matches a database column or class attribute. Defining methods named find...By..., count...By..., findDistinct...By, or even find...By...IgnoreCase will cause the Spring Data JPA module to infer the correct query and deliver results.

However, not all Spring Data JPA features work in Quarkus. Currently, there's no support for

- Future return type support; no async queries then

- QueryDSL API support

- Native queries – can't supply raw SQL to @Query

- QueryByExampleExecutor

With Panache!

The Panache toolkit is Quarkus' own data access API. It's similar enough to the Spring Data JPA API that if you're familiar with the latter, you can jump straight into the former.

Start by adding the quarkus-hibernate-orm-panache extension.

Still with my Anagram entity, I can have

```
@Entity
public class Anagram extends PanacheEntityBase {
    @Id
    @GeneratedValue(strategy = GenerationType.
    SEQUENCE,generator = "anagram_anagram_id_seq")
    @Column(name = "anagram_id",nullable = false)
    public Long id;

    @ManyToOne(fetch = FetchType.LAZY)
    @JoinColumn(name = "anagram_source_id")
    public AnagramSource anagramSource;

    public static List<AnagramSource> getAllAnagrams(){
        return (List<AnagramSource)findAll
        (Sort.ascending("anagram_source_text"));
    }
}
```

Hibernate *with Panache* places a lot of emphasis on removing boilerplate code and improving developer comfort. Here's how:

1. Extending `PanacheEntityBase` enriches my entity class with the following methods, among others:

   a) `find`, `list` – Use `list` for smaller datasets.

   b) `update`

   c) `delete`

   d) `persist`

   e) `stream`

   These methods turn my vanilla entity class into an Active Record – all the database operations I'll ever need will become static methods on the entity class itself. I'm using `PanacheEntityBase` here because I need to control the ID generation with my custom sequence and also because PostgreSQL is being weird. With other databases where `GenerationType.AUTO` just works, you can use just `PanacheEntity` instead.

2. I've set the fields on my entity to public access, instead of `private`. The Quarkus team recommends making fields non-private wherever possible to improve the performance of the framework.

3. I've gotten rid of the getters and setters – Quarkus will generate them on the fly.

4. In addition to the static methods that I inherit from
    PanacheEntityBase, I can now implement methods
    unique to this entity, reusing the inherited methods to

    a) Paginate

    b) Sort

I can then use my Panache entity directly wherever I want it:

```
public String generateAndSaveAnagram(String sourceText){
    String result = Scrambler.scramble(sourceText);
    AnagramSource anagramSource = new AnagramSource();
    anagramSource.setAnagramSourceText(sourceText);
    Anagram anagram = new Anagram();
    anagram.setAnagramText(result);
    anagramSource.persist();
    anagram.anagramSource = anagramSource; (1)
    anagram.persist();
}
```

Note how I'm setting the AnagramSource on the Anagram **(1),** to
conform with the foreign key expectations of the database. When all you
have is the primary key, the correct way to persist the foreign key reference
is by obtaining a proxy from Hibernate using the EntityManager. You can
get a hold of it by regular injection:

```
@Inject
EntityManager entityManager;
...
Long sourceId = ...
AnagramSource proxy= entityManager.getReference(AnagramSource.
class,sourceId);
anagram.setAnagramSource(proxy);
```

This approach avoids an unnecessary database trip to first retrieve the referenced entity.

Panache also provides repository-style options:

```
public interface AnagramRepository implements
PanacheRepository<Anagram> {
    public Anagram findByAnagramText(String anagramText){
        PanacheQuery<Anagram> result = find("anagramText",
        anagramText);
        return result.singleResult();
    }
}
```

It's basically the same features as PanacheEntity, but separated out into an interface, in the style of Spring Data JPA repositories. One difference here is that I don't inject the just repository interface; I need to implement the PanacheRepository on my entity. As a result, I lose the benefit of Quarkus generating query methods for me, but I gain more control over what my queries do. On the PanacheQuery you get a ton of methods that help you do a lot of manipulation over your query results. For now, I'm interested in just the single result.

The usage is as you would expect:

```
@Inject
AnagramSpringRepository anagramRepository;
...
public String generateAndSaveAnagram(String sourceText){
    ...
    Anagram anagram = new Anagram();
    anagram.setAnagramText(result);

    ...

    anagramRepository.save(anagram);
}
```

I think that's about it for Panache, for now. Do explore the PanacheEntityBase class and PanacheEntityRepository interface, for a look at the full power that ships with those two components.

With Reactive SQL

Finally, this right here is the way I want to write SQL from now on. Reactive programming is all about

- Scalability

- Resilience

- Message-driven programming

It's the programming model built for high-throughput, event-driven, and highly tunable architectures. Reactive SQL (rxSQL) delivers on that by letting you write high-performing database access code. You can treat the data being fetched from the database as events and react to them with event handlers. Reactive SQL (and really, most of reactive programming) is heavily based on functional interfaces – lambda functions. If you're comfortable with lambda functions in Java...still give this next section a look-see. I promise, I'll make it worth your while ;).

The Tools of the Reactive SQL Trade

Like I mentioned earlier, reactivity in Quarkus is driven by two classes from the Mutiny library: io.smallrye.mutiny.Uni and io.smallrye.mutiny. Multi. Uni is used to wrap and represent single items:

```
Uni<String> justOneString = Uni.createFrom().item("aString");
```

And you can get a Multi to represent multiple items:

```
Multi<String> listOfStrings = Multi.createFrom().iterable(List.
of("string1","string2","string3","string4"));
```

Cool? Cool. Quarkus allows you to use both classes in many different functional areas, but the usage follows a general pattern. Both of these classes provide a suite of methods that accept lambda expressions. These reactive methods will take the lambda function and apply them to the Uni or Multi, based on a fluent and reactive pattern. For some, lambda expressions are a little daunting, maybe unwieldy way of expressing logic. While they're an acquired taste, they're not complicated and they'll significantly improve the readability of your code. Check it out: I can have a method implementation like so:

```
public String  generateAnagram(String anagramSource){
    String anagram = Scrambler.scramble(anagramSource);
    logger,info("The scrambled string:"+anagram);
    return anagram;
}
```

To use this method as-is, I'll need to create an object of the class that contains generateAnagram and then use that object everywhere. If I have a class that offers methods that accept lambda functions – like the Uni class for example, I can do this instead:

```
Uni.createFrom().item("aString")
                .map(theString -> Scrambler.
                scramble(theString)) (1)
                .subscribe() (2)
                .with(successResult -> {
                        logger.info("The scrambled string:
                        " + successResult);
                },
```

```
failureResult -> {
    failureResult.printStackTrace();
}); (3)
```

What's all this then?

1. Right after creating a Uni to wrap the string "aString",
   I'm calling one of its lambda-accepting functions.
   map is a common operation found in pretty much
   every reactive and functional programming API in
   the Java world and beyond. It's in the JDK's stream
   API. So, map will accept any naked java method
   body or function call. Inside the map method, I
   expect a string to be available as a variable named
   "theString". From there, I'm using the scramble
   utility to convert the passed in string to an anagram.

2. To actually execute anything in the chain of functions of
   the reactive API, I must call the subscribe method. Any
   method call before a subscribe call is lazily evaluated –
   nothing will actually be invoked until subscribe is
   called. This is what's known as a terminating function
   in rx programming parlance.

3. The object returned by the subscribe function
   offers the with function. with accepts **two** lambda
   expressions: one for when the operation was successful;
   another for when the operation failed. As you can see,
   they're fully fledged method bodies as well. Contrast
   that with what I passed to the map function. This
   demonstrates two of the options available for passing
   lambda expressions to functions. It can be a very
   succinct function call like Scrambler#scramble; or a full
   method body like what I've supplied to with.

How's that for an introduction to lambda expressions and reactive programming? For rxSQL, these are the flavors of Java lambda functions you'll need to get comfy with:

- **Consumer:** a lambda function that accepts arguments and doesn't return any value. The lambda functions I passed to with are examples of consumers. They each accept arguments (a string object and an exception object respectively) but don't return a value.

- **Function:** a lambda function that accepts arguments and returns a value. map accepts only functions. Data is fed in from the preceding function item and I apply the scramble function to that data, returning the result for the next step.

- **Supplier:** a supplier doesn't accept arguments, but returns a value

With rxSQL, there are going to be a lot of other reactive types, typically based on the Uni and Multi classes. Also bear in mind that for single row results, you'll be dealing with some variant of Uni; for multi-row results, you'll be dealing with a variant of Multi. In some scenarios, it might be useful or even necessary to convert a Uni to a Multi and vice versa, so stay frosty!

To begin, I'll add the quarkus-reactive-pg-client; there are specific extensions supporting reactivity for specific database vendors. Currently, only MySQL, PostgreSQL and DB2 have reactive client support. My data source is already configured; I need to make just a couple of property changes to support reactive SQL:

```
quarkus.datasource.reactive.url =
vertx-reactive:postgresql://localhost:5432/anagrams (1)
quarkus.datasource.jdbc=false (2)
```

1. I've had to replace the standard Quarkus JDBC url property with this reactive-specific version.

2. I've had to disable basic JDBC. Raw JDBC and rxSQL currently cannot coexist enabled for the same data source.

From here on, I get to roll my own SQL statements:

```
@Inject
PgPool reactivePgPool; (1)
...
public List<AnagramResponse> findAllAnagramsBySourceId(long id){
        return reactivePgPool.preparedQuery("select * from
        anagram where anagram_source_id = $1")          (2)
                .execute(Tuple.of(id)) (3)
                .onItem()
                .produceMulti(rows -> Multi.createFrom().
                iterable(rows)) (4)
                .emitOn(executor)  (4a)
                .onItem()
                .apply(anagramRow -> {
                    logger.info("Anagram text is " +
                    anagramRow.getString("anagram_text"));
                    return AnagramResponse.fromRow(anagramRow);
                })                  (5)
                .subscribe()
                .asStream()         (6)
                .collect(Collectors.toList()); (7)

}
```

What I'm doing here should be thought of as individual, high-performace steps of a process:

1. I obtained an instance of `io.vertx.mutiny.`
    `pgclient.PgPool` client (`io.vertx.mutiny.`
    `pgclient.MySQLPool` for MySQL). This is the entry
    point into the rx SQL world.

2. I use the pool object to prepare an SQL query.
    The `$1` notation is a positional marker for supplying
    query parameters. This way, I've indicated that I'll
    be supplying a single query parameter.

3. The `execute` method is where I get to supply my
    optional query parameter. The `onItem` method
    is where I kick off the processing of any probable
    results from the query.

4. The `onItem` function produces a `Uni` of that wraps
    the output from the operation before it. In this case,
    onItem will give me a `Uni<RowSet<Row>>`, a `Uni`
    containing a rowset of rows. Because I'm expecting
    multiple rows from this query, I've decided to call
    the `produceMulti` function on the `Uni` produced
    by the query. This function allows me to pass in a
    lambda function that I can use to split the `Rowset`
    object that I get from executing the query.

    (a)   optionally, I can specify a custom `executor`
           to process the results on multiple threads,
           for a performance boost on a large number of
           results

5. For each row/item that I produce from the
    `produceMulti` function, I log the value of one column
    from the SQL query. I also create an instance of
    `AnagramResponse`. For this, I just call a static function
    I've added to the `AnagramResponse` class to create

an instance from a Row object. It's important to pay attention to the type of object you're going to have available inside your lambda function.

6. All the previous steps properly arranged, I call the subscribe method. Remember: without a call to subscribe or some other terminating function, none of the previous steps will be executed. Here, I want my subscription to yield a java Stream.

7. From my stream, I can then gather the results into a list, using standard JDK stream collectors.

Part of the beauty of the fluent API of reactive flows is how you can easily parallelize parts of the processing – what I did with emitOn. Underneath all this (even without the emitOn), This addresses a major deficiency of the standard JDK Streams feature: you can't specify a custom threadpool. Vert.x and Mutiny will efficiently manage threads for the reactive message flow, as well as being able to split the processing across multiple cores if available. Quarkus can handle reactive types natively, so I could just avoid **AnagramResponse.fromRow** step altogether and return a raw Uni . The Quarkus runtime will do all the unpacking behind the scenes and send the JSON response to the client:

```
public Uni<List<AnagramResponse>>
findAllAnagramsBySourceId(long id){

                    ...
    .apply(AnagramResponse::fromRow)
    .onItem()
    .apply(anagramResponse -> {
        logger.info("Anagram response" + anagramResponse);
            return anagramResponse;
        })
    .collectItems()
    .asList();
```

I'm supplying the AnagramResponse#fromRow function with a different style, to the apply function, but it's still a lambda-style function call. Following that, I still want to print the generated AnagramResponse, but I return the object unmodified and send it down the chain to be collected with collectItems.

If this feels like the Streams API in the stock JDK, you're not far off – they're really close in feel. Without getting into too many specifics, one key difference between JDK streams and the reactive code: Streams are pull-based, while reactive code is push-based. In this example, the query results will be pushed into the handling code.

One thing to note is that you currently can't combine reactive SQL and standard JDBC, for the same data source. So you'll need to configure quarkus.datasource.jdbc=false for each data source you want to interact with reactively. I have seen whispers of removing this barrier in pull requests on the Quarkus repo, so I envisage this might not be a thing for long.

With the rxSQL API, I can control the rate at which new rows come in with backpressure. I can add error handlers and other custom logic as part of handling the results from the query. Behind the scenes, there's efficient task switching that happens to make this a very efficient use of CPU cycles. All told, you wind up with a super scalable, resource-efficient SQL business logic. But wait! There's more!

Reactive ORM with Hibernate

Yass! There's currently *experimental* support for reactive sql with Hibernate. It goes a little something like this: first, I'll add the quarkus-hibernate-reactive extension.

Then, things get *fluent*:

```
public class AnagramResource{
    ...
    @Inject
    Uni<Mutiny.Session> mutinySession  (1)
```

```
    • • •

    @GET
    @Path("/{text:[a-zA-Z]*}/anagram/{id}")
    @Produces(MediaType.APPLICATION_JSON)
    public Uni<Response> getAnagram2(@PathParam("id")
    final int anagramSourceId) throws ExecutionException,
    InterruptedException {
    AnagramResponse response = mutinySession.flatMap(
    session -> session.find(Anagram.class,
    Long.valueOf(anagramSourceId))) (2)
            .onItem()
            .ifNull() (3)
            .failWith(new IllegalArgumentException(
            "No anagram found for that Id")) (3a)
            .onItem()
            .apply(AnagramResponse::fromAnagram)(4)
            .await()
            .indefinitely();

    return Uni.createFrom()
            .item(Response.ok()
                    .entity(response)
                    .build()); (5)
    }
}
```

Woof. That's a lotta typin'! This example is a little contrived, because I'm taking extra steps to show you specific features. Here's what's going on:

1. I need to obtain a reactive instance of a Hibernate session. This already presents a minor challenge, because instances of REST resource classes are singletons by default. What this means is that the

same instance of `AnagramResource` will be used to serve multiple requests in parallel. Hibernate sessions are famously thread-unsafe, so they can't be shared between parallel requests. The only alternative is to configure Quarkus to provide a new REST resource object per request. That's strike one.

2. With the injected ORM session, I can reactively execute a query. Pretty straightforward.

3. The resulting `Uni` offers a `ifNull` function to handle scenarios where no results are available for an operation.

   3a. Should there be no results, I can use the `failWith` function to supply an appropriate exception.

4. I then apply my transformation function, converting `Anagrams` returned by Hibernate, to `AnagramResponses` that I'll be sending in the HTTP response. The `await` method is another way of terminating the reactive flow. With this method call, I indicate that I'll wait for the completion of the execution of steps before this; I have the option to specify a timeout, or wait `indefinitely`, as I'm doing here.

5. Finally, because I want control over the HTTP response being returned, but I also want to use the reactive Mutiny API, I build a `javax.ws.rs.core.Response` object. I then wrap the `Response` object in a `Uni` of its own. Quarkus is going to be very chill about the whole thing.

So that's rxSQL[5] in a nutshell. And now, we've come to the end of my second favorite part of this book? *Noooooooo...*

---

[5]Honorary mention to Spring Data's `ReactiveCrudRepository` – rxSQL *with* an ORM layer.

NoSQL Data Sources

SQL and relational database management systems (RBDMS) are great for the majority of use cases. They're especially well-suited for analytical work, known as Online Analytical Processing (OLAP). With OLAP, you get to select rows based on any filter criteria you want: complex reporting, rollups, and so on. When you need fine-grained access to data, SQL is your Man Friday.

When you don't need fine-grained access, just fast, constant time retrieval of data on a large scale, you go NoSQL. If you're new to the concept, think of a NoSQL database as a gigantic, highly scalable, and available Hash table. This is the kind of storage you want for large-scale data use cases like gaming and media serving. Really, anything where you want to be able to access large-scale data quickly. Call it Online Transaction Processing (OLTP). You can store literally anything in there and retrieve it by a key. Some key differentiators of NoSQL are

- **No schema**: An RDBMS will need you to define a rigid schema – a collection of tables, columns, sequences, and so on that define the structure of your data storage. A NoSQL database doesn't need that much upfront work. To start using a NoSQL database, all you'll really need is a table. After that, you can store objects in it, with any number of fields and any internal structure. You don't need to know too much about the data upfront is what I'm saying.

- **Performance at scale**: For an RDBMS to start serving millions of hits, you need to carefully plan your database – the queries, the indices, partitioning tables, and so on. The underlying storage needs to be tuned for throughput and reliability. With NoSQL, you really only need to worry about how much compute capacity you'll need; in a cloud environment, your cloud provider will take care of the scalability and resource optimization.

- **No query language**: There is no standard query language (yet) for NoSQL. It's right there in the name – *no* Structured Query Language.[6] The access API is highly vendor-dependent.

There are a couple of players in this space: Neo4J, MongoDB, Redis, and a couple others. They usually can sit in the cloud; you're just going to be responsible for managing the installation. A cloud service provider could also provide NoSQL databases as a managed service, so yeah, probably go with that instead. I'm going to pick a "random" cloud provider and demonstrate how to use NoSQL in Quarkus.

With AWS DynamoDB

DynamoDB is AWS's NoSQL offering. In addition to the features you'd expect from a good NoSQL database, AWS offers

- Full service management. You'll never need to manage a server, back up your own data, or security patch anything.

- Your data can be encrypted at rest.

- Cross-region replication of your data, for fault tolerance.

- Backup and recovery of data.

- Configurable content expiry.

---

[6]This is just a happy coincidence; NoSQL is generally used to mean "Non SQL", or "Not Only SQL", according to IBM.

I'll start by adding the DynamoDB Quarkus extension, as well as the RestEasy Mutiny extension to support asynchronous DynamoDB clients:

```
mvn quarkus:add-extension -Dextensions=quarkus-amazon-dynamodb,
resteasy-mutiny
```

I could use my actual AWS account to configure an AWS-deployed DynamoDB instance and then connect to it from my local machine. I could also just run DynamoDB as a docker container on my local machine:[7]

```
docker run --publish 8000:8001 amazon/dynamodb-local
-jar DynamoDBLocal.jar -inMemory -sharedDb -port 8001
```

This docker command will

1. Pull the latest official DynamoDB image named amazon/dynamodb-local to your local Docker repository and attempt to start a local DynamoDB container.

2. Expose port 8001 on the container using **publish**, mapping port 8000 on your host machine to the container's 8001.

3. Process the arguments you supply to configure the DynamoDB container. The **DynamoDBLocal jar** file is what processes the flags that come after it. Don't worry; the file is bundled with the image.

---

[7]You can also run DynamoDB from a JAR file provided by AWS. The Docker approach is just more manageable and testable.

4. Instruct the DynamoDB instance to keep all its data
    in memory with **inMemory**. Should you terminate the
    container, all the data is lost. Use **-sharedDb** so that
    the in-memory data is shared between all clients
    that connect to this instance of Dynamo. With
    persisted data, you can use **-dbPath** to point to the
    location of the database file (named **shared-local-
    instance.db** by default) on subsequent startups.

5. Configure DynamoDB to listen on port 8001 for
    connections, using **port**; 8000 is the default, I just
    want to shake things up a bit.

With this successfully completed, go to http://localhost:8000/shell
to view the interactive shell bundled with Dynamo. Figure 5-2 shows what
you should see.

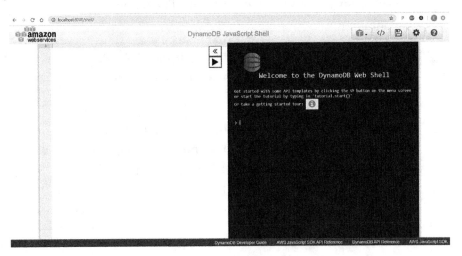

Figure 5-2. *The bundled JavaScript shell for interacting with*
DynamoDB

From this console, you can interact with the database with the AWS DynamoDB JavaScript API. There's also an actual studio where you can design your table models and so forth. Download it here. Check it out in Figure 5-3, it's pretty sleek.

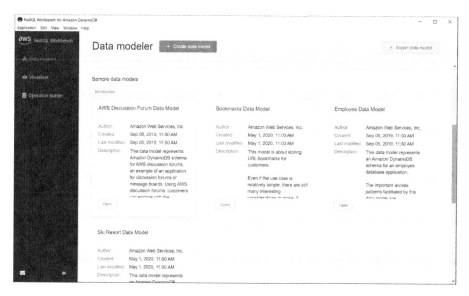

Figure 5-3.   *The landing screen of the DynamoDB data modeler*

I prefer the data modeler. I'll go to set up a connection to my local running instance of Dynamo; in the top left corner, click the **Operation Builder ➤ Add Connection** page as seen in Figure 5-4.

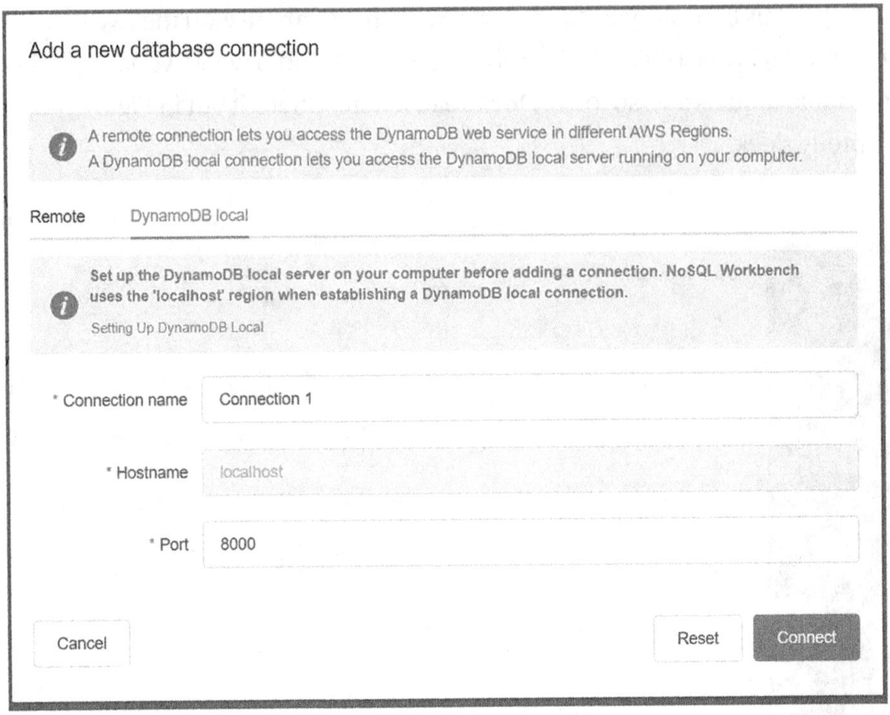

Figure 5-4. Add a local DynamoDB connection. Remote databases are right next to it

Manage Your DynamoDB Data Model

There is the database, and then there are the entities you're going to store in it. Fundamentally, there are three tiers of data to deal with:

- **Table:** The logical grouping of the entities. Just like in an RDBMS, you need a primary key. For my Anagram app, I will need two tables: Anagram and AnagramSource.

- **Item**: The actual entity, analogous to a row in a RDBMS. This is the "value" in the key-value hashmap analogy. My Anagram app will consist of items of the Anagram type as well as the AnagramSource.

- **Attribute**: The fields of the entity; what would be columns in an RDBMS. Remember, for a NoSQL database, there are no "column" restrictions. You can add as many attributes as you want to an item after the fact, with almost no consequence. Some items can have some attributes, some can be missing them, while some have other completely different attributes. It's all fine. This can be a scalar variable – integer, string, boolean, y'know, the "flat" variables. It can also be a whole object, with its own attributes.

I plan to store my entities as JSON objects; so it's easy to predict what it'll look like in storage. An Anagram:

```
{
  "id": 123974,
  "anagramText": "eve"
}
```

Now to jam all this stuff into Dynamo. I'll start with creating a schema on the Data Modeler page. Hit "Create Model" and you should see something like Figure 5-5.

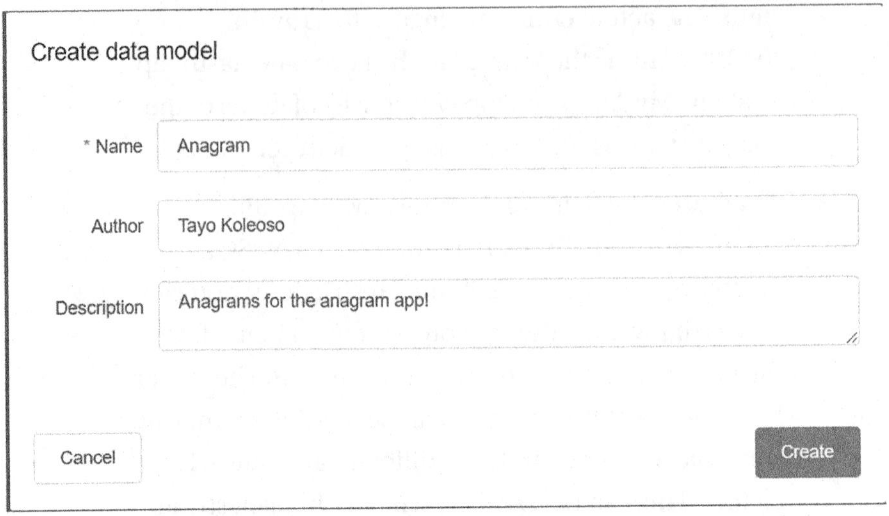

Create data model

* Name	Anagram
Author	Tayo Koleoso
Description	Anagrams for the anagram app!

Cancel   Create

Figure 5-5. Creating a data model for my Anagram app

Next, I'll create a table to hold my anagrams as in Figure 5-6.

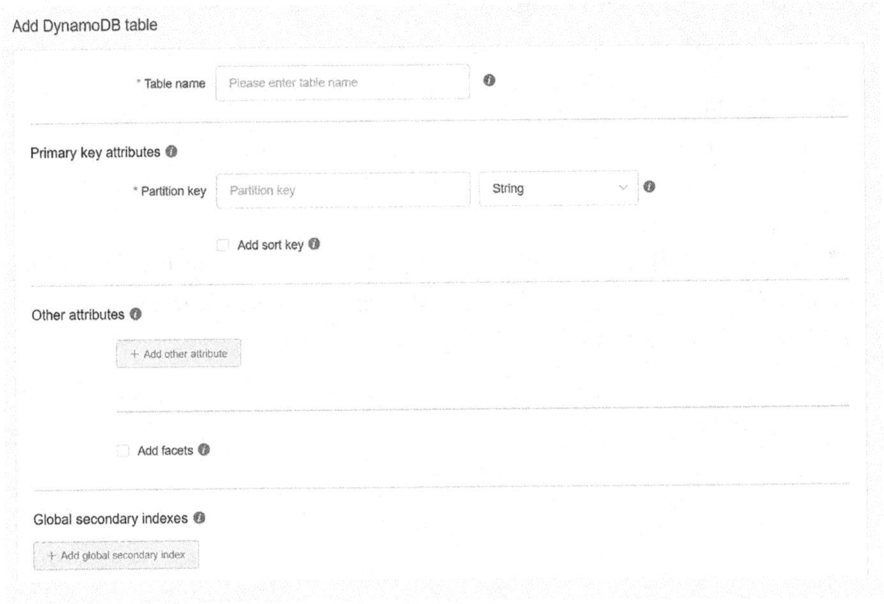

Add DynamoDB table

* Table name   [Please enter table name]   ⓘ

Primary key attributes ⓘ

* Partition key   [Partition key]   [String   ⌄]   ⓘ

☐ Add sort key ⓘ

Other attributes ⓘ

[+ Add other attribute]

☐ Add facets ⓘ

Global secondary indexes ⓘ

[+ Add global secondary index]

Figure 5-6. Defining a table for my anagrams

In here, I'm going to supply:

1. The name of the table, "anagram".

2. The primary key or "Partition key" in DynamoDB-speak. This is what I'll use to pull objects out of Dynamo. I'm choosing id from the Anagram class for this property. Which field you select for this purpose is one of the most important design decisions you'll make in the design of your NoSQL access.

Finally, I'll need to commit my data model and its table to Dynamo. On the Visualizer page, hit the "Commit to DynamoDB" button. It'll prompt you to select or configure a button for the connection:

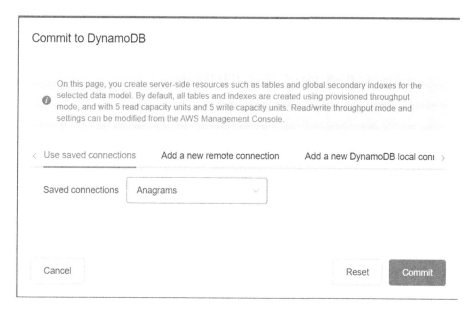

Figure 5-7. *Committing the data model to DynamoDB*

Now, let's configure access to this NoSQL database.

Configure DynamoDB in Quarkus

First, I'll pull in the AWS Java SDK for DynamoDB:

```
<dependency>
    <groupId>software.amazon.awssdk</groupId>
    <artifactId>url-connection-client</artifactId>
</dependency>
```

Per AWS, there are the following properties that need to be set for DynamoDB connectivity:

- The AWS region that your DynamoDB instance will be running in. For Quarkus, use `quarkus.dynamodb.aws.region`.

- The security details. There are a couple of options supported by AWS and how you configure them in Quarkus depends on what you choose.

  - `quarkus.dynamodb.aws.credentials.type` controls what the credential type turns out to be.

  - `quarkus.dynamodb.aws.credentials.type=static` will require you to set `quarkus.dynamodb.aws.credentials.static-provider.access-key-id` and the `quarkus.dynamodb.aws.credentials.static-provider.secret-access-key` properties. These correspond to the access key and secret access key properties that you will get from Amazon when you sign up for an AWS account. Don't worry about this for local development.

- `quarkus.dynamodb.aws.region=default` will look for the access key and secret access key in the following order in your environment:

  - `aws.accessKeyId` and `aws.secretKey` as Java environment launch variables.

  - `AWS_ACCESS_KEY_ID` and `AWS_SECRET_ACCESS_KEY` as operating system variables, corresponding to the respective key credentials.

  - The key credentials present in a file at *~/.aws/credentials* in your machine.

  - The key credentials can be delivered by the AWS EC2 metadata service. The EC2 metadata service is a read-only service that provides metadata to EC2 instances.[8] Included in that metadata are your credentials; all AWS SDKs are hard-coded to check the metadata service's endpoint before any outbound service call.

For your local machine development pleasure however, only the following properties are necessary:

- `quarkus.dynamodb.endpoint-override=http://localhost:8001`, corresponding to the exposed port on your (hopefully) running container.

- `quarkus.dynamodb.aws.region=us-east-1`. You can use any valid AWS region; it doesn't matter which you pick for local development.

---

[8]EC2 is short for Elastic Compute...2, a type of server machine that AWS provides on demand.

- `quarkus.dynamodb.aws.credentials.type=static.`
  Consequently

  - `quarkus.dynamodb.aws.credentials.static-provider.access-key-id=anything-goes`

  - `quarkus.dynamodb.aws.credentials.static-provider.secret-access-key=dummy-val`

That done, I can now get to the codin'.

CRUD in DynamoDB

The AWS DynamoDB SDK supports three flavors of connecting to the database:

- Low level

- Document-based

- High level/ORM

The high-level API is the most convenient, with a suite of annotations that map to structures in your DynamoDB database, just like you'd expect from an ORM framework. All three APIs convert your method calls into HTTP requests sent to the database for execution. Additionally, they all transparently handle cryptography, handling retries and other convenience facilities.

At the time I'm typing *these words*, Quarkus is based on the v2 of the AWS SDK which is still under development. The Document and ORM flavors aren't supported yet, so you get just the low-level API. The good news is that v2 introduces non-blocking I/O, improved streaming capabilities and your choice of HTTP client API – JDK or Apache HTTPClient.

Interacting with DynamoDB at a low level uses these classes primarily:

- `software.amazon.awssdk.services.dynamodb.model.GetItemRequest` for retrieving data from the database

- software.amazon.awssdk.services.dynamodb.model. PutItemRequest for adding data to the database

- software.amazon.awssdk.services.dynamodb.model. UpdateItemRequest for updating items

- software.amazon.awssdk.services.dynamodb.model. PutItemRequest for deleting items

- software.amazon.awssdk.services.dynamodb.model. AttributeValue for defining metadata about the attributes you need to CRUD in the database

And now, for my next trick, I'm going to CRUD with the low-level DynamoDB API.

Add an item to DynamoDB:

```
@Inject (1)
public void dynamoAdd(DynamoDbClient dynamoDbClient,Anagram
anagram){
    Map<String, AttributeValue> anagramItem = new HashMap<>(); (2)
    anagramItem.put("id", AttributeValue.builder().n
    (anagram.getId()).build()); (3)
    anagramItem.put("anagramText", AttributeValue.
    builder().s(anagram.getAnagramText()).build()); (4)
    PutItemRequest request = PutItemRequest.builder()
            .tableName("anagram")
            .item(anagramItem)
            .build(); (5)
    PutItemResponse putItemResponse = dynamoDbClient.
    putItem(request); (6)
    logger.info("operation response metadata
    "+putItemResponse; (7)
    }
```

What sorcery is this?

1. I inject an instance of `software.amazon.awssdk.services.dynamodb.DynamoDbClient`, the access point to my locally running instance of Dynamo. ArC will supply a thread-safe instance of the client object as an argument to my method.

2. I prepare a `HashMap` of `String` to `AttributeValue`. This is the map that will hold the attributes of the items I want to commit to DynamoDB.

3. I set the `id` attribute, with the `n()` method on the `AttributeValue` builder object. It's...an interesting API, definitely an acquired taste. See, you need to specify the type as well as the name of the attribute that you need to set. The DynamoDB SDK team chose the first letters of types as their method names. So, n here means I'm setting a numerical field. Bold choice of API convention for sure.

4. I set the `anagramText` attribute, using the `s()` method to indicate that this is a `String` field.

5. I build a `PutItemRequest` with the map of attributes that constitute a complete Anagram entity. It's at this point I indicate the database table this put request should go to.

6. I then pass the `PutItemRequest` to the `putItem` method on the `DynamoDbClient`.

7. `putItem` returns a `PutItemResponse`, from which you can pull a bunch of useful metadata about the table and the operation.

Retrieving an item from Dynamo? Here you go, buddy:

```
@Inject
public void dynamoGet(DynamoDbClient dynamoDbClient, String
anagramId){
    Map<String, AttributeValue> anagramItem = new HashMap<>();
    anagramItem.put("id", AttributeValue.
    builder().n(anagramId).build()); (1)
    GetItemRequest getItemRequest = GetItemRequest.builder()
              .tableName("anagram")
              .key(anagramItem)
              .attributesToGet("anagramText").build(); (2)
    GetItemResponse item = dynamoDbClient.getItem
    (getItemRequest); (3)
    String anagramText = item.getValueForField("anagramText",
    String.class); (4)
    item.item(); (5)
}
```

Here's what I'm up to:

1. I built the map of AttributeValue to hold my query parameters. Here, I'm interested in searching just by the anagramId.

2. I built a GetItemRequest to hold the table and the attribute I'm interested in retrieving.

3. The injected instance of DynamoDbClient, always at the ready, will use getItem to execute the request.

4. I then get the specific attribute I want.

5. Or, I get the whole item.

To update an item in the database:

```
@Inject
public void dynamoUpdate(DynamoDbClient dynamoDbClient,Anagram
anagram String newAnagramText) {
        Map<String, AttributeValue> anagramItem = new
        HashMap<>();
        Map<String, AttributeValueUpdate> newAnagramAttributes =
        new HashMap<>(); (1)
        AttributeValueUpdate updateAnagramText = Attribute
        ValueUpdate.builder()
                .action(AttributeAction.PUT) (2)
                .value(AttributeValue.builder()
                .s(newAnagramText).build()) (3)
                .build();
        AttributeValueUpdate brandNewAttribute (4) =
        AttributeValueUpdate.builder()
                .action(AttributeAction.ADD)
                .value(AttributeValue.builder()
                .s(anagram.getAnagramText()).build())
                .build();
        newAnagramAttributes.put("anagramText",
        updateAnagramText);
        newAnagramAttributes.put("oldAnagramText",
        brandNewAttribute);
        anagramItem.put("id", AttributeValue.
        builder().n(anagram.getId()).build());
        anagramItem.put("anagramText", AttributeValue.
        builder().s(anagram.getAnagramText()).build());
        UpdateItemRequest updateItemRequest = UpdateItem
        Request.builder().attributeUpdates(newAnagramAttributes).
        tableName("anagram").key(anagramItem).build(); (5)
```

```
UpdateItemResponse response  = dynamoDbClient.
updateItem(updateItemRequest);
logger.info("Update successful: "+response.
sdkHttpResponse().isSuccessful()); (6)
}
```

Okay, things get a little bit spicier with the update operations. The intent of this method is to update an anagram entity with a new value for anagramText. It will also add a brand new attribute to the selected item, named oldAnagramText. Walk with me:

1. In addition to the AttributeValue map that I need to supply for Dynamo to be able to find the target item, I'm now supplying a map of AttributeValueUpdate. The update operation depends on the values I set on objects of this type.

2. So, first I build the AttributeValueUpdate object to handle the update of the existing field. Setting action to AttributeAction.PUT is what makes the update click.

3. I still need to pass an AttributeValue object to the AttributeValueUpdate, to account for the content of the new data.

4. Then I build another AttributeValueUpdate to handle the creation of a brand new attribute on the existing item. Setting action to AttributeAction.ADD is the clincher here. This is one of the things that sets NoSQL apart. In the SQL world, this is analogous to creating a new column in a table as part of an insert; only, that column will apply to just a single row – invisible to the rest. Not possible with an RDBMS eh?

5. After building maps containing all the data that I need to transmit, I build an `UpdateItemRequest` that I will feed to the DynamoDB client.

6. I can then execute with the `updateItem` method on `DynamoDbClient`. Following that, I can check the status of the update with `isSuccessful` on `sdkHttpResponse`. Remember: All these method calls are wrappers around HTTP interactions with DynamoDB. The API just translates the HTTP response into convenience methods.

DynamoDB supports batch models of all the CRUD operations as well. Bon appetit!

Transactions

Transactions: You're gonna need 'em. A data operation transaction is what provides the ACID that gets your code to an elevated state:

- **A**tomicity: When you mark any sequence of method calls as transactional, they all must execute successfully as one or fail as one. Any failure in the chain should trigger an "undo" of the calls before the failure point, as well as rolling back any data changes made prior to the failure. All or nothing.

- **C**onsistency: Any transactional method should be able to guarantee that the data changes being made to a given data source obey the rules that data source has in place. For example, an insert can only be successful if it doesn't violate any referential integrity constraints set up in the data source – like primary key-foreign key relationships. Sounds like a no-brainer, yeah?

- **I**solation: A transactional operation should protect the data being operated on from concurrency-related corruption.[9] So problems like the following can be avoided:

  - **Dirty reads**: One thread reading uncommitted data that was created by a different thread concurrently.

  - **Non-repeatable reads**: One thread reading the same data twice and getting different values each time, because another thread is operating on the same data.

  - **Phantom reads**: One thread reading data that "disappears" or ceases to exist after it has been read, typically because another thread is operating on the same data source concurrently.

- **Durability**: A transactional operation must ensure that data that has been committed to the data source stays committed – even in the event of a systemic failure like disk or power failures.

Implicitly, every update you make to a database occurs as a transaction, at least as far as the database server layer is concerned. It's just that the scope of the implicit transaction is very narrow to the point where it doesn't provide too much benefit. Talking about transactions at the application layer requires talking about *boundaries*. A boundary is the chunk of your code that you want to wrap in a transaction. It's the part of your code where you use transaction APIs to buy yourself the protections

---

[9]There are a few other isolation concerns that I'm not covering here. Check out my LinkedIn Learning course on concurrency and data access. Vlad Milhacea also goes into more detail about the various ways data access can go wrong in a concurrent access situation.

of ACID. The ACID guarantee is something that a transaction manager will help you, broker, in partnership with a data source (**read**: your data source needs to support specific transaction semantics, for you to be able to rely on it). Things get even spicier when your application is distributed. Managing transactions across physically or logically separate data sources introduces the need for the disparate data sources[10] to coordinate individual operations. Not all data sources support this.

And now, because you've stayed with me this far, here's a little ad-break:

Figure 5-8. *"Welcome to Borkus!". They're already here. "Uhhh...Woof!"*

---

[10]Take note of the fact that I'm using the phrase "data source" and not database – you can get transactions out of JMS brokers, AMQP brokers, and more. It's not just a database thing, and Quarkus supports it all.

Quarkus Transactions

Quarkus provides transaction support by way of the Java Transaction API (JTA). Gotta love them standards, man. JTA provides two models for implementing transactions:

- **Declarative** using the `javax.transaction.Transactional` annotation

- **Programmatic** using the `javax.transaction.UserTransaction` interface

These two models cannot be combined – you'll get an `IllegalStateException` if you try.

There's a third framework for transactions in Quarkus, called Software Transactional Memory (STM); it is based on Narayana (bet you can't say that fast, 5 times). STM is an intriguing proposition for transaction management. Traditionally, transaction state is made durable by way of storing the transaction data in, well, *durable* storage. This introduces performance overhead that is avoidable in many situations. STM is a transaction management framework that isn't too strict on the **d**urability part of ACID. Built for high-performing environments, STM can give you a lot of bang for your buck; removing the cost of persisting transaction metadata in RAM gives all of the performance boost you would expect from constant-time, non disk I/O-bound memory access.

For now, we focus on traditional transaction management with JTA. I'll start with adding the `quarkus-narayana-jta` extension.

Declarative Transactions

It's simple: ~~we kill the Batman~~ I add @Transactional to wherever I want ACID:

```
@GET
@Path("/{name:[a-zA-Z]*}/scramble")
```

```
@Produces(MediaType.APPLICATION_JSON)
                    @Transactional(value=Transactional.
                    TxType.REQUIRED,rollbackOn=
                    {SQLException.class,IOException.class})
public ConversionResponse generateAnagram(@
PathParam("name") final String nameToScramble){

    ...

}
```

Applying @javax.transaction.Transactional to this method transparently initiates a transaction boundary. All the method calls along the chain of this method execution also get the ACID guarantee, being part of this transaction *boundary*. I also could have applied this annotation to the parent class of this method, to add transactionality to all the methods in this class.

Generally, it's encouraged to apply this annotation as close to the top of an execution chain as possible. As you can see here, I'm applying it to a REST resource method. With regard to the options for this annotation

a) **REQUIRED** here stipulates that a transaction *must* be started on entering this method, or an existing one can be used. It's also the default. There are a couple of other options in JPA that dictate how the transaction manager should propagate transactions. The sexiest one in my opinion doesn't exist in JTA. It's the NESTED option, available only in Spring. This option makes it so that a so-decorated method can act as a savepoint. If any subsequent method calls fail as part of that transaction, the transaction is only rolled back to the last savepoint. Pretty sweet.

b) **rollbackOn** tells the transaction manager
which exceptions should cause a rollback of
previously executed database operations. By
default, JTA will roll back when a subclass of
RuntimeException is thrown. No automatic
rollbacks on checked exceptions, like IOException
and *gasp*, SQLException! Conversely, there's the
dontRollbackOn attribute – "don't roll back on these
exceptions".

That's it! A couple of things to be aware of with @Transactional:

- You can't apply it to lifecycle methods like
  @PostConstruct or @PreDestroy.

- You can't apply it to static methods.

- It only delivers on the A, C, and D in ACID. You cannot
  configure **I**solation on this annotation – dirty reads,
  phantom reads, and so on are entirely possible with
  this annotation.

That last point is crucial – with just the @Transactional annotation, you
have no expectation of read consistency in a concurrent scenario. Also be
wary of mixing I/O calls – it's a code smell. By this, I mean that combining say a
web service call and a database call inside a method marked @Transactional
could become a problem, depending on how you order the calls:

```
@Transactional(value=Transactional.TxType.REQUIRED,rollbackOn={
SQLException.class,IOException.class})
    public void combinedIOCalls(@PathParam("name") final
    String anArgument){
        writeDataFromDb();
        longRunningCallToWebService();
    }
```

Putting both `writeDataFromDb` and `longRunningCallToWebService` as part of the same transaction boundary could create problems. When the transaction boundary is entered, the database connection and other resources allocated to that transaction are held for the length of that method call. Take too long and you can slowly deplete the connection pool and other scarce resources.

Consistency in Concurrency

If you're a fan of peace of mind and sleeping at night, you probably want to guarantee that different threads won't see different things when looking at exactly the same data source. You need to configure the isolation levels of your transactions. Because you can't do this with JPA's `@Transactional`, you'll need to go to the data source to provide the "I" in ACID. Configure the `quarkus.datasource.jdbc.transaction-isolation-level` to one of the five available options:

- `none`: You don't want read consistency.

- `read-uncommitted`: Allows read access to data that hasn't been committed. It's very permissive and has the lowest burden. It also allows dirty, phantom, and non-repeatable reads. Sooo, no.

- `read-committed`: This allows access to only committed data, preventing dirty reads. You're still susceptible to phantom and non-repeatable reads.

- `repeatable-read`: Prevents dirty and non-repeatable reads. You're still liable to experience phantom reads. This is the third highest level of isolation, with an increased degree of protection overhead.

- `serializable`: This option is the highest level of
  read isolation, guaranteeing protection against dirty,
  phantom, and non-repeatable reads. This is at the cost
  of concurrent access – synchronization is how this
  mode protects read access. Only one thread will be able
  to access the data table at a time. Any others must wait
  their turn, so, not a great choice for scalability.

You can also configure a transaction timeout, within which all threads
must complete their transaction business:

```
quarkus.transaction-manager.default-transaction-timeout = P75S
```

It too uses that weird-patterned `Duration` class. In this example, I've
set the timeout to 75 seconds.

The isolation level you choose is one of the more crucial choices you'll
make when configuring the data source access for your application. In a
serverless deployment, for example, things can quickly fall apart with the
wrong sort of isolation. Each run of your serverless function is effectively
a single thread – remember, serverless functions shouldn't maintain state
in themselves. An overly permissive isolation level means that multiple
hits to your serverless function, accessing the same database, will lead to
corrupt data. Choose an expensive but thread-safe option, and you will
bottleneck your serverless function, causing it to run longer than it needs
to. A long-running serverless function will cost you more money in timing
costs; increased RAM and CPU costs are also going to become an issue.
You've got to get it juuuust right, like Goldilocks.

Database Update Locking

You can decide on how much protection you want to guarantee your
concurrent writes, on a query-by-query basis using row-level locking.
Consider the `find` method on the `PanacheEntity` class:

```
@Entity
@Table(name = "anagram_source")
public class AnagramSource extends PanacheEntityBase {
    @Id
    @GeneratedValue(strategy = GenerationType.AUTO)
    @Column(name = "anagram_id", unique = true,nullable = false)
    public Long id;

    public String value;

    public static AnagramSource findByValue(String value){
        return (AnagramSource) find("value",value,
        LockModeType.PESSIMISTIC_READ);
    }
}
```

Providing a LockModeType to find allows me to define the level of read consistency I'm interested in for my database read operation. As you have probably guessed, the highest level of read consistency is also the costliest. Here are the options of LockModeType:

1. OPTIMISTIC: This is a type of locking that uses a dedicated version field or column to coordinate concurrent reads of the same entity. If your entity doesn't provide a version column, expect this to not provide any protection. If you use this option in an update operation, its version number will be incremented. It prevents dirty and non-repeatable reads by using a version column on your entity class to coordinate liveness between multiple threads accessing the same data.

2. OPTIMISTIC_FORCE_INCREMENT: This rather exotic option acts like OPTIMISTIC, even when the data hasn't been updated. That means that just accessing a data in one thread makes it out of date for other concurrent access.

3. PESSIMISTIC_READ: This is a lock mode that completely prevents concurrent writes, but allows concurrent reads. Using a write lock, once a thread gets a hold of a row, it's locked for writing. Other threads that attempt to write to the same row will catch an exception; they're free to read without consequence.

4. PESSIMISTIC_WRITE: Prevents both concurrent reading and writing. Simply accessing a row prevents another thread from doing anything with it.

5. PESSIMISTIC_FORCE_INCREMENT: This is PESSIMISTIC_WRITE + OPTIMISTIC_FORCE_INCREMENT. Really strict stuff.

6. NONE: No row locking, all concurrency problems allowed.

These controls are particularly useful for preventing lost updates, a spectacularly insidious class of concurrency problems with database transactions. Lost updates occur when two threads are trying to modify the same column, of the same row in a table. By default, most database servers will be set to READ_COMMITTED isolation, meaning that two threads accessing the same row will not see each other's uncommitted updates. The problem with that is that if they're acting on the same column of the same row, only one of them can have a successful update of that column. The other thread will still "successfully" make the update, but it won't know that another thread immediately overwrote its changes. This is where choosing a locking mechanism pays off. With an OPTIMISTIC lock mode, for example, the thread that tries to update the column last will get an OptimistLockException. This will necessitate a reattempt of the transaction, if it makes sense to do so.

Programmatic Transactions

This is transaction management where you manually define the transaction boundaries and orchestrate the transaction itself. Use the javax.transaction.UserTransaction to take charge of the situation:

```
        @Inject
UserTransaction userTransaction;
...
@GET
@Path("/{name:[a-zA-Z]*}/scramble")
@Produces(MediaType.APPLICATION_JSON)
public ConversionResponse generateAnagram(@PathParam
("name") final String nameToScramble){
    try{
        userTransaction.begin();
        //your sensitive business here
        userTransaction.commit();
    }catch(IOException exception){
        userTransaction.rollBack();
    }
}
```

I can then manually demarcate the transaction boundaries with begin() and commit(). Additionally, I can manually trigger the rollback when I please.

Batch Operations

Database operations on an entity are batched by default in JPA. Calling `persist()` on your panache entity in Quarkus adds the change to a sort of queue. The changes to that entity are then batch applied when a transaction ends or before a read on that same entity. If you're on the paranoid end of things like I am, sometimes, use `persistAndFlush()` to commit your entity changes immediately. On a larger scale, you can make bulk inserts using any of the following persist options:

- `persist(Iterable<Entity>)`
- `persist(Stream<Entity>)`
- `persist(Entity[])`

These incarnations of `persist` allow you to save a `Collection`, `Stream`, or array of entities, all in one operation. You can then call `flush()` on your `PanacheEntity` right after:

```
public void generateAndSaveAnagrams(String source){
    List<Anagram> anagrams = new ArrayList<>(30);
    for(int i=0; i++; i<30){
        Anagram anagram = generateAnagram(source);
        anagrams.add(anagram);
    }
    Anagram.persist(anagrams);
    Anagram.flush();
}
```

A couple of notes on best practice:

- You should be careful to size your batches correctly: too few items in the batch and you might as well `persistAndFlush()` after each run; too many items and you risk an `OutOfMemoryError`.

243

- The length of time you spend waiting to collect items into a batch as well as the size of each item should be a factor in how you size your batches.

- The deployment context matters a lot as well: you shouldn't use serverless functions like AWS Lambda for long-running batch operations. That is not what Lambda is ideal for.

- Managing read consistency and isolation contexts becomes more important when you're running batch operations in a serverless context. Each serverless invocation of your application is essentially a thread – more concurrent invocations, more contention of row locks.

Scheduled Jobs

You're going to write a scheduled task at some point, for it is in your destiny. Yes, you, specifically. Use the quarkus-scheduler extension to get in on this action:

```
@Singleton (1)
public class TaskMaster{
    @Inject
    Scheduler scheduledTaskMaster; (2)

    @Scheduled(every="3d", delay="5", delayUnit=TimeUnit.Hours,
    identity="StopTheWorldTask")
    public void pauseAllTasks() {
        scheduledTaskMaster.pause(); (3)
    }

@Scheduled(every="4d", delay="5", delayUnit=TimeUnit.Hours,
identity="ResumeTheWorldTask")      (4)
```

```
public void resumeAllTasks() {
    if(!scheduledTaskMaster.isRunning()){
        scheduledTaskMaster.resume(); (5)
        ((SimpleScheduledTask)scheduledTaskMaster).
        checkTriggers();
    }

@Scheduled(cron="0 15 10 * * ?",identity="EveryMorning
GramGenerator")
public void generateEveryMorning(ScheduledExecution
execution (6)) {
    generateAndSaveAnagrams(reallyLongString);
    logger.info("Scheduled for: "+execution.
    getScheduledFireTime());
    logger.info("Next execution: "+execution.getTrigger().
    getNextFireTime(); (7)
    }
}
```

Here's what I'm up to over here:

1. I've marked the bean that's going to host the
   scheduled tasks a singleton, because I need just one
   instance of this bean. This doesn't really matter to
   Quarkus, by the way. The @Scheduled annotation is
   discovered by the runtime, regardless of whether the
   parent class is a CDI managed bean or not.

2. I can inject the Scheduler, the component that
   manages all the tasks in the runtime, for my own
   nefarious purposes. You don't need this in many
   cases; just in case you do though, it's here.

3. With the scheduler in hand, I can manually pause all tasks.

4. @Scheduled is going to be the most common use case of this API. I can configure every to specify the interval of runs, delay to specify a wait before the first run of this method, delayUnit for the unit of measurement of delay, and a unique name for this scheduled task. I can also specify a cron-format schedule for the interval of execution. This cron schedule can be supplied as a property from application.properties as well.

5. I could also resume the scheduler, after pausing it. This doesn't mean that any suspended tasks will be run immediately, so I can manually trigger the execution of all scheduled tasks with checkTriggers.

6. I can obtain metadata about a specific task run from the provided ScheduledExecution object; from there, I can log some useful info, like the next time this task is to run.

For more advanced use cases, you can turn to the quartz extension which lets you use the Quartz library in your Quarkus app. Additionally, if you're coming from the Spring framework world, Quarkus supports Spring Scheduled Jobs.

Now this is all well and good for traditional use cases, but if we're talking cloud and serverless, this approach might not be necessary. AWS Lambda, for example, can be easily configured as a scheduled task; Microsoft Azure also supports step functions on a schedule.

Security

How about we use database-stored credentials to authorize *and* authenticate access to our web services? Sure JWT is nice, especially in a distributed, cloud-computing world – you can combine JWT with OAuth,[11] for example. But sometimes, you just need trusty old JDBC. More so if you're migrating your existing "legacy" APIs to Quarkus. Here's how SQL-backed security works in Quarkus.

Quarkus supports JDBC-backed authentication and authorization in many ways you'd expect. However, there's currently no support for Soteria, the Jakarta EE standard on security.[12] One place I am super impressed is the ORM-based support for authentication. This has the trademark sleekness and opinionated approach to features that I adore about Quarkus. Check it out.

Here's a schema definition for a credential database that covers your standard authentication and authorization needs:

```
CREATE TABLE user (
    user_id integer NOT NULL,
    user_name character varying(100) NOT NULL,
    password_hash character varying(500) NOT NULL
);

CREATE SEQUENCE user_user_id_seq
    AS integer
    START WITH 1
    INCREMENT BY 1
    NO MINVALUE
    NO MAXVALUE
    CACHE 1;
```

---

[11]Check out the Quarkus OAuth module.

[12]I know right! They've finally gotten around to standardizing the plethora of security specifications for enterprise Java!

```
INSERT INTO user (user_id, user_name, password_hash) VALUES
(1, 'mynameiswhat', '$2a$10$nvPeasph1j4cPex3rUY4n.dbCs.
af3UUNLvnrf5FY.H39i5b5qh6e');
INSERT INTO user (user_id, user_name, password_hash) VALUES
(2, 'mynameiswho', '$2a$10$KxXhooqEAtyZ3pZSudtTjeOfxObfPpMnaXfU
2xmI3FtUq/v4fas/S');

ALTER TABLE ONLY users
    ADD CONSTRAINT users_pkey PRIMARY KEY (user_id);
CREATE TABLE role (
    role_id integer NOT NULL,
    role_name character varying(25) NOT NULL
);
CREATE SEQUENCE role_role_id_seq
    AS integer
    START WITH 1
    INCREMENT BY 1
    NO MINVALUE
    NO MAXVALUE
    CACHE 1;

ALTER TABLE ONLY role ALTER COLUMN role_id SET DEFAULT
nextval('role_role_id_seq'::regclass);

ALTER TABLE ONLY role
    ADD CONSTRAINT role_pkey PRIMARY KEY (role_id);

INSERT INTO role (role_name) VALUES ('VIP');
INSERT INTO role (role_name) VALUES ('HOYPOLOI');

CREATE TABLE user_role_mapping (
    user_id bigint NOT NULL,
    role_id bigint NOT NULL
);
```

```
ALTER TABLE ONLY user_role_mapping
    ADD CONSTRAINT role_id_ref FOREIGN KEY (role_id) REFERENCES
    role(role_id);

ALTER TABLE ONLY user_role_mapping
    ADD CONSTRAINT user_id_ref FOREIGN KEY (user_id) REFERENCES
    user(user_id);

INSERT INTO user_role_mapping (user_id, role_id) VALUES (1, 1);
INSERT INTO user_role_mapping (user_id, role_id) VALUES (2, 1);
```

This schema definition provides

1. A role table that lists named roles that describe the authorizations of users in this service.

2. A user table that holds the users that will have access to the application in general.

3. A user-role mapping table that connects the user and role tables. This way, a single user can have multiple roles; a single role obviously will be mapped to multiple users. A proper many-to-many relationship.

4. Roles rows for roles "VIP" and "HOYPOLOI".

5. Two users named "mynameiswhat" and "mynameiswho", both with password "password". A very safe and strong password that you should *totally* put on a sticky note next to your work station.[13] Five out of five doctors recommend this.

---

[13]Editor's note: Do **not** do this! What is wrong with you?!

Bueno! Now, I create my AuthenticatedUser JPA entity that will stitch users and their roles together. What will my AuthenticatedUser entity look like?

```
@UserDefinition (1)
@Entity
@Table(name = "user")
public class AuthenticatedUser extends PanacheEntityBase {
    @Username (2)
    @Column(name = "user_name", nullable = false, unique =
    true)
    public String username;

    @Password (3)
    @Column(name = "password_hash", nullable = false, length = 500)
    public String password;

    @Roles (4)
    @ManyToMany (5)
    @JoinTable( (6)
            name = "user_role_mapping",
            joinColumns = @JoinColumn(name = "user_id",
            referencedColumnName = "user_id"),
            inverseJoinColumns = @JoinColumn(name = "role_id",
            referencedColumnName = "role_id"))
    public List<Role> roles = new ArrayList<>();
}
```

Here are the pieces at play:

1. io.quarkus.security.jpa.UserDefinition marks this entity class as the "user" class that will identify the principal trying to connect to your service.

2. `io.quarkus.security.jpa.Username` marks this field as the "user name" field of the entity.

3. `io.quarkus.security.jpa.Password` designates this field as the password field. The framework expects this field to hold the hash of the password, not the plain text version. BCrypt is the default hashing function.

4. `io.quarkus.security.jpa.Roles` will use this field to hold a list of entities that map to the roles or groups that the parent entity has.

5. Because of the many-to-many relationships that I've set up between the `user` and `role` tables using the `user_role_mapping` table, I need the `@ManyToMany` annotation here.

6. Along with the `@ManyToMany` annotation, I need to use the `@JoinTable` annotation to establish the relationship between the three tables.

Here's the Role entity:

```
@Entity
public class Role extends PanacheEntityBase {

    @Id
    @GeneratedValue(strategy = GenerationType.
    IDENTITY,generator = "role_role_id_seq")
    @Column(name = "role_id",nullable = false, unique = false)
    public Long id;

    @Column(name = "role_name",nullable = false)
    @RolesValue
    public String name;
```

```
@ManyToMany(mappedBy = "roles")
List<AuthenticatedUser> users;
}
```

`io.quarkus.security.jpa.RolesValue` marks this field as the name of the role. The value in this field is what an authenticated entity will present as its role. @ManyToMany annotation establishes the other side of the three-way connection between user, user_role_mapping, and role.

Finally, I'll throw this little piece in there to handle creating new users:

```
public static void add(String username, String password, Role
role) {
    AuthenticatedUser user = new AuthenticatedUser();
    user.username = username;
    user.password = BcryptUtil.bcryptHash(password);
    user.roles.add(role);
    user.persist();
}
```

Quarkus provides the BcryptUtil#bcryptHash method to help generate the hash value for use in the password field. Now let's protect a resource. I'll add the following property to enable BASIC authentication for my endpoint:

```
quarkus.http.auth.basic=true
```

Now I need to enforce security on an endpoint. I'll use a GET endpoint that returns an image:

```
@GET
@Path("/hello-image")
@Cache(maxAge = 30)
@Operation(summary = "Returns an image")
@Produces("image/jpg")
```

```
@RolesAllowed("VIP")
public Response helloImage() throws InterruptedException,
ExecutionException {

    ...
}
```

The presence of @RolesAllowed makes Quarkus kick in an authentication requirement for that endpoint. Any attempts to hit that endpoint will enforce the need for credentials supplied via the Authorization HTTP header. With all this in place and some user records in the database, I can attempt to hit the endpoint in a browser. That attempt will open up the authentication dialog that looks something like Figure 5-9.

Figure 5-9. *The Mozilla authentication dialog box*

All I need to do is fill in the credentials and I'm granted access. For a more "technical" test, I'll use SoapUI. This requires me to have generated the bearer token to fill into the Authorization HTTP header as in Figure 5-10.

Figure 5-10. Testing my REST authentication in SoapUI

Tip   You can get the value for the Authorization header from your browser. Open the network console in your browser and attempt to hit the secured endpoint. That will yield a dialog box like the one in Figure 5-6. Fill it out and proceed to success. In the network tab of your console, you can then view the request payload and copy the authorization header off it, to use inside the API testing tool of your choice.

Regardless of your testing tool of choice, you should get a successful authentication response from your application, given the correct authentication credentials.

And that, ladies in gentlemen, is how you do data in Quarkus. There are a many other data-relate cool things that I couldn't include in this chapter. I highly recommend you check some of them out, including:

- Pub-sub to PostgreSQL database with reactive SQL. PostgreSQL has the capability to notify you of changes to the database and data using the reactive connection.

- Debezium also allows you to stream changes from your database upward into your Quarkus application.

- So. Much. Cloud. Quarkus provides support for a lot of cloud-based data services like Amazon's SQS, SNS and S3.

  - For integration to cloud services though, I recommend you go through Apache Camel instead of connecting through naked Quarkus. It opens up a wider variety of options and gives more bang for buck.

CHAPTER 6

Test Quarkus Applications

Okay, don't start snoring just yet! I know testing isn't the sexiest thing, but we must talk about it. Because "testing is important" and "it's the hallmark of mature code and software engineers," or "if you don't write about testing, we'll launch you out of a cannon and set a flamethrower to your book's manuscript.[1]"

Quarkus' testing support is based on JUnit version 5, JUnit Jupiter. JUnit 5 is quite a different animal from JUnit 4, so even for a grizzled veteran like yourself, a primer might be helpful.

JUnit Primer

The fundamental *unit* of the J*Unit unit* testing framework (see what I did there?) is the @Test annotation:

```
public class BasicJUnit{
    @Test
    public void testOrdered1(){
        Assertions.assertEquals(2,1+1,"1 and 1 is not 2 ??");
    }
}
```

---

[1]Editor's note: We said no such thing ;).

© Tayo Koleoso 2020
T. Koleoso, *Beginning Quarkus Framework*, https://doi.org/10.1007/978-1-4842-6032-6_6

The @Test annotation is going to run the annotated method and Assertions.assertEquals will validate that the result of that computation is what is expected. Otherwise, the string message is displayed as a failure message. There's a whole host of tooling that JUnit provides; here's a small sampling of some of my favorite bits – mostly from the revamped Jupiter platform:

```java
@DisplayName(value = "A JUnit Jupiter Test Class ") (1)
@TestInstance(value = Lifecycle.PER_CLASS) (2)
@TestMethodOrder(OrderAnnotation.class)
public class SampleUnitTest {

    @BeforeEach (3)
    public void onePerTestTimeInit(){
        //run some setup before each test method
    }

    @ParameterizedTest (4)
    @Tag("tag1") (5)
    @ValueSource(strings = {"Supersonic","Subatomic","Java!"})
    public void loadValues(String values){

    }

    @ParameterizedTest
    @Tag("tag1")
    @CsvSource({
        "Olamide, Koleoso",
        "Mo, Sylla",
        "Eden, Wassiamal
    })
    public void loadValuesFromCSV(String firstName, String lastName){
```

```java
        assertNotNull(firstName);
        assertNotEquals(lastName,"");
    }

    @Test
    @Tag("tag2")
    @Timeout(value = 3, unit = TimeUnit.SECONDS) (6)
    public void testTimeoutException(){
        try {
            Thread.sleep(4000); //force a wait
        } catch (InterruptedException e) {
            // TODO Auto-generated catch block
            e.printStackTrace();
        }
    }

    @RepeatedTest(3)    (7)
    @DisplayName("It's a repeat!")
    public void testDuplicateRequests(RepetitionInfo
    repetitionInfo){
        //test logic that will be executed repeatedly for the count
    }

    @Test
    @Order(1)  (8)
    public void testOrdered1(){
        Assertions.assertEquals(2,1+1,0,"1 and 1 is 2");
    }

    @Test
    @Order(2)
    public void testOrdered2(){

    }
```

```
@AfterEach (8)
public void oneTimeCleanup(){
    //perform cleanup tasks after each @Test method has run
}
}
```

1. @DisplayName to help IDEs render your JUnit test classes with a fancy display name of your choice, instead of just the class name.

2. @TestInstance to configure how JUnit should handle instances of your test class. You can have one instance of the test class for all the available @Test methods, so you can share instance variables between each method; or you can have a new instance per test method, so that no sharing (or corruption) of state occurs between test runs.

3. @BeforeEach to execute some code before each run of any @Test method present in the class. @BeforeAll is an alternative that will execute just once, before all the available @Test methods run. You can have both in the same unit test class.

4. @ParameterizedTest to designate a test method as one that accepts parameters. You can then use one of many @*Source annotations to designate where the values can be supplied from – ranging from a fixed list of String here to a CSV file. The given test method will be run for each value available. There's even @MethodSource that you can use to supply values from a method!

5. @Tag to categorize your test methods with the
    configured names. This becomes useful when you
    need to exclude some unit tests from a test run or
    include only some tests.

6. @Timeout to validate response times. Use this
    annotation to validate that the test case doesn't
    exceed the configured timeout.

7. @RepeatedTest to execute the given test method a
    configurable number of times. This is particularly
    useful in the microservice world where it's
    important to validate the behavior of an API
    endpoint that might receive repeated or "phantom"
    requests. Being RESTful means that one must
    guarantee that an idempotent endpoint behaves
    idempotently.

8. @Order and @TestMethodOrder together to
    orchestrate between multiple @Test methods,
    deciding the order in which they should execute.
    This might encourage one to blur the lines between
    unit, integration, and behavioral testing. Make of
    that what you will ;).

9. @AfterEach to execute the method after each
    invocation of a @Test method in the unit test class.
    Also available: the @AfterAll annotation to execute
    a method once after every @Test method has
    completed.

So, that's what I consider the JUnit starter kit for microservices. Now to
add a little bit of Quarkus flavor to things!

Unit Testing

To test in Quarkus at all, you'll need the quarkus-junit5 extension. It's the only extension in the ecosystem that isn't available via the quarkus maven plugin (you can't add the extension with quarkus:add-extension as at the time of this writing). You'll need to add the POM.xml entry manually:

```
<dependency>
    <groupId>io.quarkus</groupId>
    <artifactId>quarkus-junit5</artifactId>
    <scope>test</scope>
</dependency>
```

To accommodate JUnit 5, you'll need to update the Maven Surefire plugin in your POM.xml. If you started this project using any of the Quarkus tooling, you'll find the version config property in the properties section of your POM.xml. At this time, 3.0.0-M4 is the latest version:

```
<surefire-plugin.version>3.0.0-M4</surefire-plugin.version>
```

Otherwise, you can add the plugin afresh yourself:

```
<plugin>
    <artifactId>maven-surefire-plugin</artifactId>
    <version>${surefire-plugin.version}</version>
    <configuration>
        <systemProperties>
          <java.util.logging.manager>org.jboss.logmanager.
          LogManager</java.util.logging.manager>
        </systemProperties>
    </configuration>
</plugin>
```

Finally, I'll add test engines, a prerequisite for Maven to run any unit tests I define:

```xml
<dependency>
    <groupId>org.junit.jupiter</groupId>
    <artifactId>junit-jupiter</artifactId>
    <version>5.6.2</version>
    <scope>test</scope>
</dependency>
<dependency>
    <groupId>org.junit.vintage</groupId>
    <artifactId>junit-vintage-engine</artifactId>
    <version>5.6.2</version>
    <scope>test</scope>
</dependency>
```

The junit-jupiter dependency will pull in all I need for JUnit 5 tests; junit-vintage-engine is there to allow me run the JUnit 4 unit tests.

Pro Tip   The example classes in this book generally aren't using interfaces. These aren't production or real-world classes. In your actual day-to-day programming, you should be coding to interfaces and, consequently, testing against **interfaces**. This way, your tests aren't tightly coupled to the classes. Brittle tests are a chore; don't write your beans this way!

Unit Test CDI Beans

Now for some Quarkus magic. Since Quarkus fundamentally operates in a dependency injection context – CDI – being able to inject your CDI (or Spring)-annotated beans is a basic need. Let's take this CDI bean from earlier:

```java
import io.quarkus.vertx.ConsumeEvent;
import io.vertx.axle.core.Vertx;
import io.vertx.core.eventbus.Message;

@RequestScoped
public class EventBusMessageRecipient{

    @Inject
    Vertx vertx;

    final Logger logger = Logger.getLogger(EventBusMessageRecip
    ient.class.getName());

    ...

    @ConsumeEvent("two-way-message")
    public EventMessage receiveTwoWayMessage(String message){
        logger.info("Received two-way message "+message);
        EventMessage response = new EventMessage();
        response.setMessage("Message received");
        return response;
    }
    ...
}
```

To be able to unit test this class, you need to be able to obtain a managed instance of it inside our unit test class. This is where the @QuarkusTest annotation comes in. This annotation bootstraps the Arc CDI engine; it'll then provide any managed beans you've defined, along with any dependencies those beans use – with some limitations[2]:

```
import io.quarkus.test.junit.QuarkusTest;
...
import org.junit.jupiter.api.Assertions;
import org.junit.jupiter.api.Test;

@QuarkusTest (1)
public class ExampleResourceTest {

    @Inject
    EventBusMessageRecipient eventBusBean;

    @Test (2)
    @DisplayName("Test for two-way messaging with the Vert.x
    event bus")
    public void testEventBusTwoWay(){
        String message = "message to send";
        EventMessage eventResponse = eventBusBean.
        receiveTwoWayMessage(message);
        Assertions.assertNotNull(eventResponse);
        Assertions.assertEquals("Message received",
        eventResponse.getMessage());
    }
}
```

---

[2]I talk more about this a little later.

Here's what's going on:

1. @QuarkusTest is a JUnit 5 extension that starts up
    an instance of your application to make your whole
    Quarkus application available within the unit test.

2. With the application running, you can now inject
    your CDI bean and validate the assumptions.

Note that the JUnit imports are from the `org.junit.jupiter` package, indicating the JUnit 5 dependency; this will become an important point shortly.

All that's left now is to run the unit test. Now, I love the JUnit integration in the VS Code IDE, but there is an idiomatic route to run tests with Maven:

```
mvn test
```

This kicks off my unit tests and shows me the test results.

Note   This isn't a pure unit test. A "pure" unit test will isolate your CDI bean code from any of its dependencies. Anything that your CDI bean depends on should ideally be mocked using mocking frameworks like Mockito and PowerMock.

Unit Test CDI Components

The Quarkus + JUnit 5 Combo is just splendid for unit testing standard CDI beans that *you* created – CDI beans here mean beans you've annotated with @Named, @RequestScoped, and @Singleton. Where things get dicey is where you have to unit test components. By components, I'm talking about filters, interceptors, exception mappers, and so forth. This isn't supported by the Quarkus unit testing framework. You also can't inject components with @Context with the Quarkus unit tester. But fear not! Arquillian to the rescue!

Unit Test with Arquillian

Arquillian is the premier testing platform for CDI and JavaEE componentry; it's been around for a while and even the Quarkus platform uses it for internal testing. Arquillian provides a JUnit harness that allows us to bootstrap an embedded JavaEE application server as part of a JUnit unit test class; this gives you the full strength of the JavaEE runtime in a portable testing framework. Neato!

So, let's say I have a JAX-RS exception mapper that I've configured for my Quarkus app:

```
import javax.ws.rs.core.Response;
import javax.ws.rs.ext.Provider;
import javax.ws.rs.ext.ExceptionMapper;

@Provider
public class JAXRSExceptionMapper implements
ExceptionMapper<Exception>{
    @Override
    public Response toResponse(Exception exception) {
        return Response.serverError().status(400).build();
    }
}
```

This is an exception handler that will trap all exceptions thrown in my Quarkus app and return an HTTP-400 status code to the service requester. I'll now introduce Arquillian into the mix:

```
<dependency>
    <groupId>junit</groupId>
    <artifactId>junit</artifactId>
    <version>${junit.legacy.version}</version>
    <scope>test</scope>
</dependency>
```

```
<dependency>
    <groupId>org.jboss.arquillian.junit</groupId>
    <artifactId>arquillian-junit-container</artifactId>
    <version>${arquillian.version}</version>
    <scope>test</scope>
</dependency>
```

As at the time of this writing, there's no official Arquillian support for JUnit 5; junit.legacy.version needs to be the highest JUnit 4 version: 4.12; for Arquillian, I'll use the latest at this point: 1.6.0.Final. Finally, I need to select the type of embedded JavaEE container that Arquillian will use for the JUnit bootstrapping; there are a few options; I'm going with the embedded Weld-EE container; it plays very well with the rest of Quarkus, based on my test drive of it:

```
<dependency>
    <groupId>org.jboss.spec</groupId>
    <artifactId>jboss-javaee-7.0</artifactId>
    <version>1.1.1.Final</version>
    <type>pom</type>
    <scope>provided</scope>
</dependency>
<dependency>
    <groupId>org.jboss.arquillian.container</groupId>
    <artifactId>arquillian-weld-ee-embedded-1.1</artifactId>
    <version>1.0.0.Final</version>
    <scope>test</scope>
</dependency>
<dependency>
    <groupId>org.jboss.weld</groupId>
    <artifactId>weld-core</artifactId>
```

```
      <version>2.4.8.Final</version>
      <scope>test</scope>
  </dependency>
```

With this setup, I can run JUnit 4 and 5 tests in the same mvn test run. Arquillian is still sitting pretty. Configuration is done; all that's left is the actual unit test:

```
import org.junit.Test;
import static org.junit.Assert.assertEquals;
...
import org.junit.runner.RunWith;
import javax.ws.rs.core.Response;
import javax.ws.rs.ext.ExceptionMapper;
import javax.inject.Provider;

@RunWith(Arquillian.class)(1)
public class ExampleResourceTest {

    @Inject
    Provider<ExceptionMapper<IllegalArgumentException>>
    exceptionMapperProvider; (2)

    @Deployment
    public static JavaArchive createDeployment() {
        return ShrinkWrap.create(JavaArchive.class)
            .addClass(JAXRSExceptionMapper.class)(4)
            .addAsManifestResource(EmptyAsset.INSTANCE,
            "beans.xml");
    }

    @Test
    public void testMapper(){
        ExceptionMapper<Exception> mapper =
        exceptionMapperProvider.get(); (4)
```

```
    Response response  = mapper.toResponse(new Exception("A
    generic failure"));
    assertEquals(400, response.getStatus());
  }
}
```

Pay attention to the import of @Test and assertEquals: they must be from org.junit.Test and org.junit.Assert respectively. These are the packages from the legacy version of JUnit. For the test itself, here's what's up:

1. Using the @RunWith annotation from JUnit 4, I use the Arquillian runner class.

2. Injecting javax.inject.Provider is how I get a hold of my JAX-RS providers inside the unit test; this is an idiomatic way of obtaining specific providers in the CDI context. Anything annotated with @Provider can be obtained this way.

3. This is a little splash of Arquillian sorcery over here: @Deployment comes from the Arquillian kit; the point of the entire createDeployment method is to package artifacts of interest into a dynamically generated JAR file. For most testing needs, this is all mostly boilerplate code. The crucial part of all of this is the addClass method. Use this method to package the classes you'll need to inject into your unit test. There's also an addClasses method to add multiple classes in one go.

4. I then retrieve an instance of my specific provider using the get method on the javax.inject. Provider interface.

As normal, I hit the ol' `mvn test`, but this time, I'll supply a profile parameter so that my Arquillian-based test dependencies kick in:

```
mvn test -Parquillian-glassfish-test
```

This kicks off the JUnit 4 + Arquillian-based unit test. My JUnit 5 test dependencies are still configured and intact.

Quarkus Mocking

To achieve purity of test, you can mock out the dependencies in your code. A pure unit test should execute only the methods inside the target class; injected code and dependencies will not be invited to the testing party. Quarkus uses CDI magic to provide mocking for CDI beans; check it out.

Given my CDI bean:

```
import io.quarkus.vertx.ConsumeEvent;
import io.vertx.axle.core.Vertx;
import io.vertx.core.eventbus.Message;

@RequestScoped
public class EventBusMessageRecipient{

    @Inject
    Vertx vertx;

    final Logger logger = Logger.getLogger(EventBusMessage
    Recipient.class.getName());

    ...

    @ConsumeEvent("two-way-message")
    public EventMessage receiveTwoWayMessage(String message){
        logger.info("Received two-way message "+message);
        EventMessage response = new EventMessage();
```

```
        response.setMessage("Message received");
        return response;
    }
    ...
}
```

I can mock it out like so:

```
@Mock
@RequestScoped
public class MockEventBusMessageRecipient extends
EventBusMessageRecipient{
    public EventMessage receiveTwoWayMessage(String message){
        EventMessage response = new EventMessage();
        response.setMessage("Mock Message received");
        return response;
    }
    ...
}
```

io.quarkus.test.Mock designates this class as a mock. @QuarkusTest
will inject the mock instead of the real bean:

```
import io.quarkus.test.junit.QuarkusTest;
...
import org.junit.jupiter.api.Assertions;
import org.junit.jupiter.api.Test;

@QuarkusTest
public class MockEventBusMessageRecipientTest {

    @InjectMock
    EventBusMessageRecipient eventBusBean;
```

```
    @Test
    public void testEventBusTwoWay(){
        String message = "message to send";
        EventMessage eventResponse = eventBusBean.
        receiveTwoWayMessage(message);
        Assertions.assertEquals("Mock Message received",
        eventResponse.getMessage());
    }
}
```

When you combine this with the @AlternativePriority feature, you can have a suite of beans that can be transparently substituted for one another, based on priority. Now, this isn't an all-out replacement for the mocking powerhouses like Mockito and PowerMock, but it's a nice supplement. Speaking of Mockito...

```
import io.quarkus.test.junit.QuarkusTest;
...
import org.junit.jupiter.api.Assertions;
import org.junit.jupiter.api.Test;
import io.quarkus.test.junit.mockito.InjectMock;
import org.mockito.Mockito;

@QuarkusTest
@TestInstance(value = Lifecycle.PER_CLASS)
public class EventBusMessageRecipientTest {

    @InjectMock
    EventBusMessageRecipient eventBusBean; (1)

    @InjectMock
    @RestClient
    HttpBinServiceDAO binServiceRestClient;(2)
```

```
@InjectMock
AnagramRepository anagramRepository; (3)

Anagram anagram = new Anagram();

@BeforeAll
public void init(){
    anagram.setAnagramText("scrambledText");
    Mockito.when(eventBusBean.receiveTwoWayMessage(
    "Hey y'all!")).thenReturn(new EventMessage("Hello
    yourself!")); (4a)
    Mockito.when(binServiceRestClient.
    postAnything("Say something")).thenReturn(new
    HttpBinAnythingResponse("Hi, Drake!"); (4b)
    Mockito.when(anagramRepository.count()).
    thenReturn(231); (4c)
    PanacheMock.mock(Anagram.class); (5)
    Mockito.when(Anagram.findById(100)).
    thenReturn(anagram); (5a)
}
...

}
```

With the quarkus-junit5-mockito extension installed, I've been able to

1. Mock out my actual EventBusMessageRecipient.

2. Mock out my MicroProfile REST client for the HTTP Bin REST service. Note that I still had to decorate it with the @RestClient annotation from MicroProfile.

3.   Mock out my Panache repository.

4.   Use raw Mockito to define the behavior I want for the three mocks I injected earlier.

With the quarkus-panache-mock extension, I can use the PanacheMock class to mock out my Panache entities, like the Anagram class . The way @ InjectMock works, it'll replace the target bean with either a mock that you supply with @Mock, or a dumb stub. The stub or mock will replace the real deal throughout the test.

Tip   Version 1.5 of Quarkus introduces @InjectSpy, with the quarkus-junit5-mockito extension. This introduces support for Mockito spies: when you just need to ensure that a method was called, but not necessarily executed on a bean, use @InjectSpy.

Integration Testing

Okay, I know that my individual classes work because I can unit test them. How about the entire application? How can I know that my API endpoints will respond the way I expect? How do I know that my individual CDI beans and other components all integrate correctly and work together to produce the results I want? Integration testing, baby!

An integration test is going to activate your code and anything your code depends on – within limits. Your application could depend on Quarkus-provided components and CDI-provided components. It could also depend on a database, an external web service, and other black box systems; an integration test is the type of test that can help you activate that whole string of dependencies. You could also engage selected execution paths by mocking out specific components in a test class. Now, deciding how deeply you should integration test has become a philosophical debate in the software engineering business, so I'll leave that up to you.

@QuarkusTest enables that by starting up your Quarkus application as part of a JUnit test. Past that, all you have left to do is execute your API endpoints. For this, most people turn to Restassured.

Restassured is arguably the most popular API testing and validation library with an extremely robust API that you can use to

- Validate the structure and content of an API's HTTP response

- Work with both JSON and XML

- Work with Scala and Kotlin

- Integrate your tests with JUnit, Cucumber, SpringMVC, and much more

- Validate JSON and XML schemas

Here's what it looks like in action:

```
import io.restassured.RestAssured;

...

@ParameterizedTest
@CsvSource({
    "Olamide, Koleoso",
    "Eden, Wassiamal
})
public void validate_that_valid_jwt_is_generated(String
firstName, String lastName) {
    RestAssured.
      .when().get("/hello-world/{firstName}/{lastName}/
      generate-token-for",firstName,lastName)
      .then()
        .statusCode(200);
}
```

This simple snippet invokes my running Quarkus application – started by the @QuarkusTest – and validates that for the given endpoint, the expected status code is returned. This is a basic example of what can be done with Restassured. There's a lot of power in that library, maybe even too much, especially if I'm looking to avoid introducing yet another library to my project. Well, friend, I could just inject a MicroProfile client into my unit test. Given a MicroProfile client interface like so:

```java
@RegisterRestClient(baseUri = "http://localhost:8080/")
public interface HttpBinServiceDAO{

    @GET
    @Path("/hello-world/{firstName}/{lastName}/generate-token-
    for")
    @Produces("text/plain")
    CompletionStage<byte[]> getTokenRx(@PathParam("firstName")
    String firstName,@PathParam("lastName") String lastName );

    @GET
    @Path("/hello-world/{firstName}/{lastName}/generate-token-for")
    @Produces("text/plain")
    Response getToken(@PathParam("firstName") String
    firstName,@PathParam("lastName") String lastName);

    @POST
    @Path("/hello-world/validate-token")
    @Produces("text/plain")
    Response validateToken(String jwtString);

}
```

I can now inject my client into a unit test like I would any other class that uses a web service client:

```
@QuarkusTest
public class IntegrationTest {

    @Inject
    @RestClient
    UnitTestClient unitTestClient;

    String firstName;
    String lastName;
    ...
    @Test
    public void validate_that_valid_jwt_is_generated() {
        Response response = unitTestClient.getToken(firstName,
        lastName);
        Assertions.assertEquals(200, response.getStatus());
    }
}
```

The two unit tests above are functionally similar, but the latter achieves the same end without an additional library. Heck you could call it an advantage that this could easily help integration-test the MicroProfile client, period. When you combine the REST client injection with the test ordering that JUnit provides, you could construct some very powerful integration tests:

```
@TestMethodOrder(OrderAnnotation.class)(1)
@TestInstance(value = Lifecycle.PER_CLASS) (2)
@DisplayNameGeneration(DisplayNameGenerator.ReplaceUnderscores.
class)
public class JUnitIntegrationTest{
```

```
String generatedJWT;

...

@Test
@Order(1) (3)
@Tag("JWT")
public void validate_that_valid_jwt_is_generated() {
    Response response = unitTestClient.getToken(firstName,
    lastName);
    Assertions.assertEquals(200, response.getStatus());
    generatedJWT = response.readEntity(String.class);
}

@Test
@Order(2) (4)
@Tag("JWT")
public void validate_that_my_valid_jwt_is_valid() {
    Response response = unitTestClient.
    validateToken(generatedJWT)
    Assertions.assertEquals(200, response.getStatus());
}
```

This snippet is a rudimentary integration test that I built purely in JUnit 5. Observe:

1. @TestMethodOrder configures the ordering strategy for this unit test class. OrderAnnotation.class stipulates that the @Order annotation be used, with respect to the number supplied to it.

2. @TestInstance defines how the instance of the test class ought to be handled. Because my two test methods need to share data, I've configured this unit test class to maintain a single instance across all test method invocations.

3. @DisplayNameGeneration configures how the test cases will appear in IDEs, console output and in the test report. With DisplayNameGenerator.ReplaceUnderscores.class, my validate_that_my_valid_jwt_is_valid will be displayed as "validate that my valid JWT is valid" in Surefire's test report file and everywhere else.

4. @Order specifies the order in which the given method will execute relative to the rest.

5. @Tag helps to categorize the test methods for build-time filtering or inclusion/exclusion.

To run this integration test, I use the verify goal:

```
mvn verify
```

Hint   @QuarkusTest will start your Quarkus application for testing on port 8081 by default. You can control this behavior by configuring quarkus.http.test-port in your application.properties file. Also, you can control the profile that your tests start with using the quarkus.test.profile.

So, pick between the vanilla REST client and restassured, depending on the complexity of your integration testing needs. The complexity of your integration tests is increased by the various things that your application depends on. You could be interested in testing just the REST endpoint, and maybe a specific database integration; but that REST endpoint also injects a websocket endpoint, a Kafka client etc - a bunch of stuff that you shouldn't have to spin up to integration test just the CRUD. This is where slicing comes in.

Slicing Integration Tests

The major hassle with integration testing, in my opinion, is all the dependencies. Wanting to run an integration test usually means having to bring up the whole application and all its dependencies. This always leads to brittle integration tests and pain. The tests become more complicated to maintain than the actual product.

Slicing is a technique that helps you focus your integration tests so that you don't have to worry about bringing up the entire application and all its dependencies. Checkout this composition of a hypothetical ExampleResource REST resource class:

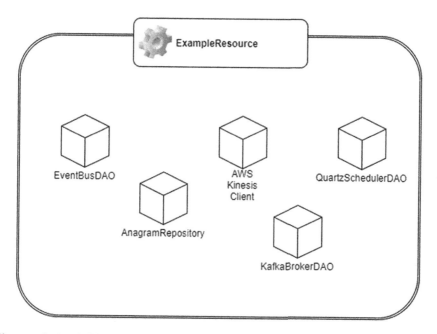

Figure 6-1. *A REST resource class and its dependent beans*

@QuarkusTest will bring up the whole application – all the REST resource classes, dependencies, the lot of them. If your testing operation is going to scale, you're not going to have a good time going on this way. With slicing, you can select the string of classes and components that you want to test together as part of an integration test. Figure 6-2 shows how the previous example could be sliced for a more focused integration test:

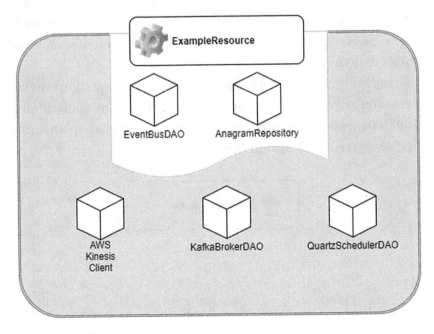

Figure 6-2.   A sliced integration test

After slicing, only the two components I'm interested in should be part of the startup of my Quarkus application.

A couple of components in the standard Quarkus toolkit let you slice to some extent. The cohort of @Mock, @AlternativePriority, @DefaultBean etc can help you achieve something close.

But, what if you want to select a precise chain of classes to devise an automated integration test case scenario? You don't need the whole thing, just one or two specific classes? If you want the Quarkus laser knife of slicing, checkout the io.quarkus.test.QuarkusUnitTest class. Check it out:

CHAPTER 6   TEST QUARKUS APPLICATIONS

```
public class SliceTest {

    @RegisterExtension (1)
    static QuarkusUnitTest runner = new QuarkusUnitTest() (2)
            .setArchiveProducer(() -> ShrinkWrap.
            create(JavaArchive.class) (3)
            .addClasses(ExampleResource.
            class,EventBusMessageRecipient.class) (4)
            .addAsResource("test-profile-application.
            properties","application.properties")); (5)
                        @Test
                        public void validate_that_valid_jwt_is_
                        generated() {
                            RestAssured
                          .when().get("/hello-world/
                          {firstName}/{lastName}/generate-token-
                          for","firstName","lastName")
                                .then()
                                    .statusCode(200);
                        }
}
```

So, a little word of caution: this is an internal Quarkus team technique
that as at the time of this writing, they're not yet advertising for external
use[3]. I've seen their internal debate about publishing this officially, so it's
very likely you'll see this in the near future. Now, what am I doing in this
JUnit test class?

1. `org.junit.jupiter.api.extension.`
   `RegisterExtension` is a Jupiter annotation that lets
   you customize the lifecycle of a test class.

---

[3] *The testing technique that "they" don't want you to know!*

2. `QuarkusUnitTest` is what I use to essentially start up a standalone, empty Quarkus application. Consider it your whole Quarkus application, minus all your classes. This is the only required bit of this code snippet.

3. The `ShrinkWrap` utility helps to portably package or "shrinkwrap" a full Jakarta EE application. Past this point, I only need to provide specific parts of my application that I'm interested in including in my integration test run. Does any of this look familiar? I hope so – I introduced the `ShrinkWrap` in the unit test section of this chapter.

4. Here, I just want my Example REST resource endpoint and the event bus message recipient implementation. I'm at liberty to include any kind of class here, as long as I need it for my integration test.

5. Another customization I can apply, is my property file. Without this step, `QuarkusUnitTest` will load the `application.properties` that I have in my application. With `addResource`, I can supply an alternate property file, and I specify that my alternate property file be treated like the standard "application.properties". You can apply this treatment to any other resource files – `import.sql`, `web.xml` etc can be overriden with this mechanism.

With all that, I'm now able to start a very narrowly focused version of my app and integration test against it. Pretty neat, huh? Here's some more neatness that "they" *do* want you to know.

Quarkus Test Profiles

You can exert even more control over your test runs with a programmatic test profiles. Here's how that looks:

```
import io.quarkus.test.junit.QuarkusTestProfile;
...
public class SampleTestProfile implements QuarkusTestProfile (1){

    @Override
    public Map<String, String> getConfigOverrides()(2){
        return Collections.singletonMap("quarkus.http.test-
        port", "8009");
    }

    @Override
    public Set<Class<?>> getEnabledAlternatives()(3){
        return Collections.singleton(AlternativeExample
        Resource.class);
    }

    @Override
    public String getConfigProfile()(4){
        return "special-test";
    }

    @AlternativePriority(1)
    public class AlternativeExampleResource extends
    ExampleResource
    ...
    }
}
```

A test profile class allows me to do a sort of last-minute customization of my test run:

1. I implement the QuarkusTestProfile interface. This interface provides default implementations of all its methods, so you don't need to implement all, or even any of them.

2. getConfigOverrides allows me to dynamically override the properties I've already set in my application.properties file.

3. getEnabledAlternatives allows me to manually specify alternatives to classes that will be loaded by my test run. It's here you can manually specify custom versions of components or mocks in general.

4. getConfigProfile will let me override the default "test" profile used by Quarkus.

Altogether, I can command and control my test run by applying my test profile:

```
@TestProfile(SampleTestProfile.class)
@QuarkusTest
public class SliceTest {
  ...
}
```

So, take control of your automated testing!

Suppress Security for Integration Tests

New with Quarkus 1.7, you'll be able to control the authentication and authorization requirements for some lucky endpoints! Start by adding the Quarkus Test Security dependency:

```
<dependency>
    <groupId>io.quarkus</groupId>
    <artifactId>quarkus-test-security</artifactId>
    <scope>test</scope>
</dependency>

<dependency>
    <groupId>io.quarkus</groupId>
    <artifactId>quarkus-elytron-security-properties-file
    </artifactId>
</dependency>
```

quarkus-test-security provides the @TestSecurity annotation; quarkus-elytron-security-properties-file is a Quarkus extension that allows you to define credentials inside your property file.

Are you thinking what I'm thinking? Let's all have a smoothie bre- oh that's not what you were thinking. Fine. Here's are some sample properties file credentials configurations:

```
#Enable the embedded credential store for the test profile
alone
%test.quarkus.security.users.embedded.enabled=true

#Allow the credentials to be stored here in plaintext instead
of encrypted (which is also an option)
%test.quarkus.security.users.embedded.plain-text=true
```

```
#For a user named "tayo-1", set the password to "password".
#This line simultaneously creates the user and sets the
password
%test.quarkus.security.users.embedded.users.tayo-1=password

#Set the role for the named user
%test.quarkus.security.users.embedded.roles.tayo-1=VIP

#Enable BASIC authentication. This is currently the only
#supported mechanism for TestSecurity
%test.quarkus.http.auth.basic=true
```

This setup configures a user ID "tayo-1", with a role "VIP" and a password of "********"[4], all in the test profile. All that's left is for me to introduce @TestSecurity to an integration test:

```
import io.quarkus.test.security.TestSecurity;
...
@QuarkusTest
class SampleSecurityTestCase {

    @Test
    @TestSecurity(authorizationEnabled = false) (1)
    void testSecurityDisabledGet() {
        RestAssured
                        .when().get("/hello-world/{username}/
                        scramble-async","tayo-1")
                        .then()
                            .statusCode(200);

    }
```

---

[4]Yeah, *real* secure, Tayo.

```
@Test
@TestSecurity (2)
void testSecurityEnabledGet() {

    RestAssured
                    .when().get("/hello-world/{username}/
                    scramble-async","tayo")
                    .then()
                        .statusCode(401);
}

@Test
@TestSecurity(user = "tayo-1", roles = "VIP") (3)
void testGetWithUserAndRole() {
    RestAssured
            .when()
            .get("/hello-world/{username}/
            scramble-async","tayo")
            .then()
            .statusCode(200);
}
}
```

Let's dig in, shall we?

1. With @TestSecurity#authorizationEnabled = false,
    I can suppress the security requirement for this endpoint,
    so I don't need to do any additional security work.

2. With authorizationEnabled = true, I can expect the
    endpoint to rightfully fail my connection request.

3. With the right username and role, I can then get a
    successful response.

At the time of *writing these words*, @TestSecurity isn't supported for native mode integration testing. You can use both HTTP Basic and Oauth at this time.

Hmm, I feel like I'm forgetting someth-.

Native Mode Integration Testing

Ahh yes, testing in native mode. All the testing I've demonstrated so far has been implicitly against a JAR-packaged Quarkus application – the so-called JVM mode. You definitely want to verify that your microservice works properly when packaged as a native application. Here's how:

```
import io.quarkus.test.junit.NativeImageTest;

@NativeImageTest
public class NativeResourceTest{
    UnitTestClient nativeImageClient;
    String firstName = "Tayo";
    String lastName = "Koleoso";

    @BeforeAll
    public void initOnce(){
        nativeImageClient = RestClientBuilder.newBuilder()
        .baseUrl(new URL("http://localhost:8081/"))
         .build(UnitTestClient.class);
    }

    @Test
    public void testJWTEndpoint(){
        Response response = nativeImageClient.
        getToken(firstName, lastName);
        Assertions.assertEquals(200, response.getStatus());
    }

}
```

@NativeImageTest designates this test class as being one for a native image. You'll notice that I'm manually bootstrapping a MicroProfile REST client, you eagle-eyed detective you. Well, native mode testing doesn't support dependency injection. What this means is that @Inject will not be able to supply dependencies. Not a huge loss; just a tad inconvenient. All that's left is to run the darn thing:

```
mvn verify -Pnative
```

This command will kick off a native image build, as well as run the native mode integration test. Bueno!

Integration Testing with TestContainers

I've been able to unit test my individual classes; I've also integration tested my components strung together. The final frontier [drum roll] is testing my application in containerized form. This is where TestContainers comes in.

TestContainers is a platform that supports all manner of integration testing against containers. It's hella powerful too; it

- Provides throwaway containerized versions of popular black box systems like databases, message queues, and buses

- Provides canned testing platform for UI integration testing

- Allows you to test your own containerization – everything from generating Docker images to creating containers straight from a Dockerfile or anything else you have

- Integrates nicely with JUnit and other testing frameworks

If you're going to truly WORP, this is a solid tool in the arsenal. It's really straightforward to use too. I'll start by adding the dependency to ye olde POM.xml:

```
<dependency>
    <groupId>org.testcontainers</groupId>
    <artifactId>junit-jupiter</artifactId>
    <version>1.14.0</version>
    <scope>test</scope>
</dependency>
```

And now, I test. Wish me luck:

```
@Testcontainers (1)
@QuarkusTest
public class ContainerIntegrationTest{

    @Container (2)
    GenericContainer containerFromDockerFile =  new
    GenericContainer(
    new ImageFromDockerfile().withDockerfile(
    Paths.get("src/main/docker/Dockerfile.native")
                                        )
                                      );

    @Container
    GenericContainer containerFromImage = new
    GenericContainer("quarkus/code-with-quarkus"); (3)

    @BeforeAll
    public void initOnce(){
        nativeImageClient = RestClientBuilder.newBuilder()
        .baseUrl(new URL("http://localhost:8080/"))
        .build(UnitTestClient.class);
    }
```

```
@Test
public void verifyNativeContainerImage(){
    Assertions.assertNotNull(containerFromImage);
    Response response = unitTestClient.
    getToken(firstName, lastName);
    Assertions.assertEquals(200, response.getStatus());
}

}
```

So, what have I done here?

1. The @TestContainers annotation is what bootstraps
   the TestContainers runtime. It allows it to start up
   and shut down its internal docker runtime; it's how
   it manages images and containers.

2. @Container helps my instance of GenericContainer
   key into the JUnit test lifecycle. TestContainers
   allows me to create a container straight from a
   supplied Dockerfile or

3. Create a container from an already existing Docker
   image. Here, I've supplied the name of the image I
   created for my local Quarkus app.

With my Quarkus app bootstrapped as part of the JUnit lifecycle,
I'm free to interact with it like any other container. In this integration
test, I'm hitting the containerized app on port 8080, because that's the
port I've exposed in the Dockerfile. There's so much more you can do
with TestContainers – unit testing your Dockerfile is the least you can
do. TestContainers will handle the startup, shutdown, and any cleanup
necessary as part of the unit test. Pretty sweet, eh?

Index

A

Ahead-of-time (AOT)
compilation, 3, 5
Amazon Web Services
(AWS), 133, 161
ArC CDI engine
avenues, 34
conditional bean supply, 38
container-managed
components, 34
custom lifecycle events, 36, 37
default beans, 37
io.quarkus.arc.ArcContainer, 34
lazy bean initializations, 35, 36
lean bean cleaning machine, 39
limitations, 40
Quarkus enriches, 35
@AroundInvoke annotation, 32
Arquillian, 267
Atomicity, 232
Azure Kubernetes Service
(AKS), 160

B

Batch operations

flush(), 243
notes, 243
persist options, 243
scheduled jobs, 244–246
BcryptUtil#bcryptHash
method, 252

C

@ClientHeaderParam
annotation, 95
Command-line interface (CLI), 171
Consistency, 232
@ConsumeEvent annotation, 129
@Context annotation, 25, 34, 35
Contexts and Dependency
Injection (CDI)
beans, 23, 24
bean scopes, 25, 26
definition, 23
Continuous integration/
continuous deployment
(CI/CD), 142
createDeployment method, 270
Cross-origin resource sharing
(CORS), 97

© Tayo Koleoso 2020
T. Koleoso, *Beginning Quarkus Framework*, https://doi.org/10.1007/978-1-4842-6032-6

Printed in the United States
By Bookmasters